DEVELOPING SUCCESSFUL GRANTS

How to Turn Your Ideas into Reality

Mike DuBose, MSW

Martha Davis

Anne Black, MS

Research Associates, Inc.
Columbia, South Carolina
www.grantexperts.com

DEVELOPING SUCCESSFUL GRANTS
How to Turn Your Ideas into Reality

© 2005 by Research Associates, Inc.

Book design by Mary E. Wall
Editing by Christine O'Brien

Research Associates, Inc.
169 Laurelhurst Avenue
Columbia, South Carolina 29210
803-750-9759
www.grantexperts.com

Printed in the United States of America

Contents

INTRODUCTION

As a grants development, evaluation, and training firm, Research Associates has trained and worked closely with nearly 20,000 individuals on how to write, find, evaluate, and administer grants. We have also written hundreds of grants with an overall success rate of 90 percent, obtaining over $200 million in funding for our clients. Not only have we learned a great deal of information about grants development from our clients and students, we have also identified many different styles and approaches to creating a successful grant proposal.

When we began to write grants more than twenty years ago, we were driven by the same needs motivating many of you—the need to purchase something for our agencies, such as a computer. When we began writing the grant proposal, we simply wrote a description of what we wanted to buy, why it was needed, and what it would do for us. Admittedly, these early proposals were unfocused, did not flow well, and probably contained poor grammar. Some of our early success was surely due to little more than beginner's luck!

Through the years, we began to understand the deficits in our early grant proposals—the same deficits common to many unsuccessful proposals today. We had no real understanding of the problems in the community, nor did we envision how our grant programs would impact these problems. Further, we failed to understand or explain how the grant proposal aligned with the larger mission of our agency. As we began to understand these fundamental differences between grantwriting and fundraising, we began to develop more and more winning proposals.

And as we refined our model for developing successful proposals based on this understanding, we began sharing our knowledge with others in our workshops and seminars. We believe it is important to assemble the components of a grant proposal in a specific, logical sequence, not only because it saves time, but also because it creates a flow within the proposal, providing information to the reader in a clear, concise manner. Our goal is to create a grant proposal that reads like a novel, moving smoothly from point to point, and so engaging that no one wants to put it down.

Whether you are juggling grantwriting in an already crowded full-time work schedule or trying to write grants in your personal time, you will benefit by reducing the frustration and time it can take to create a successful grant proposal. Our approach will help all grantwriters, regardless of focus, since grantwriting theory is the same across all fields of interest. We will help you write proposals *in the least amount of time* and in *the most logical manner.*

ABOUT THE AUTHORS

Mike DuBose, M.S.W., founder and president of Research Associates, has developed 130 large grants and more than 500 small grants totaling over $200 million with an overall success rate of 90 percent. Mike has also served as a grants administrator for more than 100 grant programs.

Having trained more than 20,000 individuals in both graduate courses and grantwriting seminars, Mike is consistently rated as outstanding by participants in his various grants development workshops. Mike serves as a field instructor for the University of South Carolina, College of Social Work, and his employment history includes positions with seven state agencies in South Carolina, grants administrator for two South Carolina governors, and executive director of the private nonprofit South Carolina Home Health Association.

Martha Davis, senior vice president of Research Associates, leads the Grants Development and Evaluation Services Divisions and is charged with expanding the company's base of operations throughout the nation. Currently responsible for the oversight of 18 regional offices strategically matched to federal grant regions, Martha supports new business development and facilitates the company's grants development projects. Under her leadership, Research Associates has secured more than $68 million in federal and state grants for the company's customers, with an overall success rate of 90 percent.

Martha is an integral part of the company's post-grant consultation and technical assistance and also directs legislative affairs on behalf of the company's grant clients. As a former executive director of a South Carolina nonprofit education fund, Martha brings unique experience as both a grant maker and grantwriter.

Anne Black, M.S., is director of special projects at Research Associates, serving as instructor for grant seminars and onsite workshops while providing oversight for all certified course curricula. As a senior grantwriter, she develops grant proposals, coordinates grants team efforts, and develops program models. Anne has coauthored numerous publications with Mike DuBose.

Anne's professional positions include a faculty appointment at the Medical University of South Carolina, director for research and evaluation at a large federally funded neighborhood healthcare center, and administrator for an inner-city Episcopal mission center providing adult daycare and Head Start programs. She has served on the board of a multicounty nonprofit providing addictions prevention, intervention, and treatment services. Anne serves as a board member for the Lexington (South Carolina) Medical Center Foundation.

THE RESEARCH ASSOCIATES LOGICAL GRANTWRITING MODEL

After many years, we have developed a unique method of ogically and in the least amount of time. Although there are many possible approaches that might be employed for grantwriting, this logic-based model has worked extremely well for us. We have achieved a success rate of 90 percent with over $200 million in funded grant proposals. Even though most grant application guidelines require that components of proposals be presented in a specific order, we recommend that you write the components in the sequence we recommend in this book and then rearrange them to comply with the application guidelines. The following paragraphs provide an overview of the twelve steps of the **Research Associates Logical Grantwriting Model**.

Step 1: Preparing for Success

Before you can successfully compete for grants, you must establish agency processes that support the grantwriting effort. We will help you determine what resources are needed and identify which potential programs complement your agency mission so you can create your agency's road map for grantwriting. We will explain why it is necessary to identify and train others to assist in the grantwriting efforts. *It truly takes a village to write a grant!*

Step 2: Finding Funding Sources

Before you write grants, you must first find them. We will solve the mystery of locating the 65,000 national funding sources awarding nearly $500 billion annually. *We will show you the money!* And once you have located these resources, what happens next? We will explain how to acquire and interpret funding guidelines—the Request for Proposals (RFP)—so you will understand *what funding sources want to "buy"* with their grant monies.

Step 3: Defining the Problem

It is critical to successful grantwriting that you adequately identify and compellingly describe the community needs your program will target. We'll suggest ten reliable methods for digging up the dirt in your community and then show you how to draft and validate your conclusions with independent statistics. We'll coach you in proven methods for developing compelling descriptions of these problems. *We will make those reviewers cry, and ultimately, they will want to give you the money!*

Step 4: Developing Program Strategies

It is important to funding sources that your program be different and creative. We'll suggest techniques for developing program strategies that will meet these criteria. Further, we'll share the seven secrets of telling your story in an engaging manner that will allow reviewers to visualize your project coming alive as they read your proposal. And throughout the process, we will suggest ways to gain extra points from reviewers, because grantwriting is like a game where *the one with the most points wins!*

Step 5: Defining Your Mission and Tasks

Once your program strategies have come together, Step 5 will guide you in developing the specific components defining the goal(s) of this grant program. These goals are the changes you are trying to achieve—*how you will make the world a better place!* We'll show you how to present your goals effectively and how to develop measurable objectives that will define success for both funders and program managers.

Step 6: Designing the Evaluation

Another key to writing a successful grant proposal is including a plan for evaluating the program so both you and the funding source will know the answer to the question, Did we succeed? While emphasizing the importance of independent program evaluation, we will explain how to establish the basis for program evaluation, with definitions related to your measurable program objectives.

Step 7: Strengthening the Proposal

In this step, we will teach you about two components that strengthen every proposal. First is dissemination of information, or telling others about your program (both what did and did not work). While this may seem like tooting your own horn, it serves a broader purpose for funders who understand that with one small investment, they may impact thousands of additional individuals. The other selling point we recommend is presenting your plan for program sustainability beyond the initial funding. *How will you keep the dream alive?*

Step 8: Managing the Program

You must convince the funding source that you have the management skills and know-how to implement and carry out the program you have described. We'll show you how to develop and present a management plan with components such as time lines to accomplish your task. With our coaching, your management plan becomes your secret weapon for convincing funders they *can trust you with their money!*

Step 9: Building the Budget

We will share our secrets for building realistic budgets that are program-driven and presented clearly. We'll help you evaluate the true cost of program operations while also demonstrating community support for your program. Using our techniques, your budgets will be strong enough to stand alone and pass reviews with flying colors. *Your bottom line will be correct!*

Step 10: Bringing It All Together

Excitement builds during this step as you bring all components of your proposal together and prepare it for presentation to funding sources. We'll share expert tips regarding your writing style and maximizing your proposal's visual appeal. We'll also consider your choice of grantwriting tools and emphasize the importance of proofreading. *"Misteaks" can be costly!*

Step 11: Finishing Touches

We will guide you through all the necessary housekeeping steps for completing a winning proposal. We offer advice about your program summary, table of contents, forms, appendices, and one more round of proofreading. We even discuss delivery of your proposal. *The model is almost complete—just one step to go.*

Step 12: Following Through

You may think proposal submission is the end of your job as a grantwriter, but it isn't. We'll explain the grants review process so you are primed and ready for two important additional steps. The first is learning to respond to funding inquiries *without losing your cool—or points.* And second is the role of political intervention, or *the art of influencing outcomes.*

RA Note: The Research Associates Logical Grantwriting Model is a proven process. These twelve steps, simple and straightforward, are a solid beginning for developing award-winning grants. For grantwriters who want to achieve more, we offer three days of detailed training in our **Certified Grant Specialist Seminar** based on this model. To learn more about this workshop and others that we offer, visit our website at **www.grantexperts.com.**

STEP 1
PREPARING FOR
SUCCESS

One of the most important facets of successful grants development for any organization is often the most ignored: establishing an organized grants development process. Many private nonprofits, school districts, universities, and government agencies are chasing grants just to pay the bills. Unfortunately, many of these organizations are unsuccessful because they lack a well-defined strategy that enhances success in finding, applying for, obtaining, and implementing grants.

In working to secure grants with more than one hundred private nonprofits, school districts, and government agencies over the last twenty years, we have observed that some organizations receive millions of grant dollars, while other agencies—often with greater financial needs—receive few, if any, grants. What is limiting the success of these organizations? Despite sending the message to employees and volunteers that grants development is extremely important, these organizations fail to develop a system that supports and rewards grantwriters. Consequently, they fail to secure grant funding.

Designing a Successful
Agency Grants Process
You Need a Road Map

What is the secret to obtaining grants? We believe the key is creating a process within your organization **before** beginning to write the first grant proposal. It is important to develop a clear, written strategy including a needs assessment of the problems or needs you plan to address, the programs you want to develop, and the items you want to purchase. A coordinated grantwriting process will reduce frustration, enhance collaboration, increase the number of grants funded, and pave the way for many new programs that otherwise could not be funded.

Here are some guidelines on how to provide the support that grantwriters and grantwriting teams need to be successful in developing grant proposals. They also address the problems and barriers that prevent many organizations from obtaining grants.

►► *Invest in the decision to pursue grants.*

Most organizations fail to see the value of investing in the resources necessary for successful grants development. Identify one individual in your organization as the **grants seeker**. Help that person gain a comprehensive understanding of the grants process by providing for formal training on how to locate grants as well as basic instruction on how to develop grants. Further, allocate a budget of at least $1,000 for the grants seeker to establish a library of grant directories and newsletters. Even a modest grants library will help identify appropriate resources from the more than 65,000 foundations, corporations, and government grant programs that award nearly $500 billion each year.

If your agency does not have a full-time **grantwriter**, consider hiring one. Organizations that employ full-time grantwriters with a focus on grants development are the most successful in obtaining grants. These positions nearly always pay for themselves within two years. Other options are to employ a part-time grantwriter or contract with a grant consultant.

►► *Establish clearly what is needed and why.*

Too often, grantwriters are forced to work from a "wish list of things to buy" rather than a cohesive plan that aligns with the organization's mission. The plan is crucial because funding sources want to know why these things are needed and how they can benefit stakeholders. Thus, you must begin by conducting a needs assessment among the various professionals in your organization. We will discuss a needs assessment of your target population in Step 3.

Conducting a staff needs assessment does not have to be a complicated process. It can be as simple as distributing a one-page form to all staff asking four questions: (1) What problems would you like our agency to address through potential grants? Rank them by priority, need, or concern. (2) What program activities would you like to develop to address the problems stated above? (3) What specific items (equipment, supplies, travel, personnel, consultants, etc.) would you like to purchase? (4) How will you contribute to the development of a grant proposal for our agency (writing, reviewing, word processing, proofing, budget development, etc.)? After responses are reviewed and organized, management and staff then work together to establish overall agency priorities.

Assessing agency needs though staff input builds a bridge and sense of ownership between the grantwriter or grants team and the professionals who will implement the grant programs. A written plan developed from the needs assessment will identify organizational goals and needs and provide a road map for the grants seeker in finding the appropriate grants.

▶▶ *Create written guidelines for grants processing.*

Your agency should develop simple, written guidelines on how a grant proposal proceeds through the organization. Establish the procedures that define how grants are identified, developed, reviewed, and approved. Assemble a decision-making committee that has the authority to expeditiously approve the development of a grant proposal. Avoid bureaucratic barriers such as requiring the board of directors to approve grant proposals. If possible, designate one trained person to coordinate the grant development process for the organization. This person should not serve as a bureaucratic roadblock but as a facilitator to guide the grantwriter(s) and other grants team members.

►► *Establish incentives as part of the grants development process.*

Too often, private nonprofits, school districts, and government agencies fail to apply the same business principles used by their for-profit counterparts to reward employees. However, the fact is people work harder and operate at higher levels of efficiency when they are rewarded and recognized for their success. Just as for-profit companies provide bonuses and incentives to individuals for outstanding work and for projects that bring in financial resources, nonprofit and government organizations must consider similar incentives to enhance grants team success. Be creative and recognize that incentives can include public recognition, cash bonuses, extra vacation time, travel to national conferences, higher salaries, and updated equipment.

One school district we know rewards educators with a 5 percent cash bonus from local funds for any grants they bring into the district. It is no surprise this district has been very successful in obtaining many beneficial grants, large and small, and has established a track record of grants success. Because of the incentives awarded for success, these educators are constantly seeking opportunities to improve their skills, and ultimately, their success.

►► *Develop grantwriting teams within your organization.*

In most organizations, grantwriting occurs in isolation. Many grantwriters prefer to work alone and resist teamwork. As a result, there is no clear process and no coordinated effort to promote working toward a common vision. Once the organizational needs assessment has been completed, identify professionals and volunteers who are interested in the **grantwriting team**. Individual involvement can range from reviewing drafts to actually writing sections of grant proposals. You'll want to identify persons with skills in writing, editing, program development, word processing, researching, and budgeting. Be sure to include staff members who have served as grants reviewers. These teams need support and training to do their jobs successfully; this is an excellent investment since they can develop more grants and bring in significantly more grant funds than individual grantwriters working alone. We'll take a closer look at grantwriting teams in the next section.

▶▶ *Involve outside agencies.*

Ideally, your agency should create an interagency grantwriting team with members from various organizations working together to write grants and share grant funds. Invite other private nonprofit agencies, faith-based organizations, school districts, schools, universities, government agencies, businesses, and community groups to work with your organization in identifying and applying for grants. Since grant notices are distributed to a wide range of organizations, these alliances will increase available funding opportunities. In addition, funding sources often prefer a partnership application to a single-agency applicant. Another bonus is that while one partnering organization may be eligible to apply for a grant, other agencies can serve as contractors for services thereby receiving some grant monies. Establish a philosophy of sharing grant monies rather than simply applying for grants alone—or worse, competing against each other. When there is collaboration, grantwriting is certain to be more successful!

Developing Successful Grantwriting Teams
It Takes a Village to Write a Grant

One of the keys to Research Associates' success has been the creation of grantwriting teams. We have assembled a group of talented individuals to identify needs and develop award-winning proposals. Grant competition is fierce, so involving a number of individuals with varying expertise, backgrounds, talents, and education creates a stronger grant proposal that will not only survive, but shine during the review process. Through the years, our firm has obtained grants worth hundreds of millions of dollars for our customers. This would not have been possible without the involvement of many individuals working in teams towards common goals.

Creating successful grantwriting teams is not an easy task, but it can be done. A grantwriter in one of our recent seminars remarked that collaboration or partnerships are best described as an "unnatural act between two consenting adults or organizations"! The point is, most grantwriters would prefer to work alone rather than involve others in the process.

Keep in mind that a successful team can't be assembled overnight, but in the long term, a cohesive team will result in more grants funded, less frustration during the development process, and a reduction in the amount of work on everyone's part during grants development. Most importantly, grantwriting teams frequently develop proposals that enhance program outcomes when implemented because their approach is more diverse than that of a solo grantwriter. This is because the team provides a much broader vision by involving more viewpoints during program design, resulting in fewer unanticipated problems during administration of the program.

There's no question that grantwriting teams are the key to success, but how do we assemble these teams and make them work? Here are some tips to guide you in creating and organizing all types of grantwriting teams—teams that write successful grant proposals.

▶▶ *Select team members from different backgrounds.*

Ensure your team is diverse. Our company staff represents different races, genders, cultures, ages, employment histories, experiences, and educational backgrounds. We all have a variety of life experiences and see our world from different points of view. For example, a person who grew up in rural poverty has different insights than an individual who was raised in an urban, middle class setting. It is also important to solicit the involvement and advice from those in the target population. Funding sources also encourage involvement from diverse community members. Their involvement will result in a grant proposal that is more realistic and more likely to be successful.

▶▶ *Solicit organization and community support.*

Maintain a positive or "can do" attitude that a grantwriting team will be beneficial and that a strong team can be assembled. There are community volunteers and members of your organization who can contribute greatly, if they are identified and asked to serve. *Despite Research Associates' reputation for obtaining grants, the local public schools our children attend have never approached us to review or assist with any grant proposals.* Remember, there are people like us in your community who want to help and who have useful skills. It simply takes time and a positive attitude to locate and enlist those individuals.

▶▶ *Seek team members with different expertise.*

Our goal is to create a team that will bring a variety of expertise to the table, thus reducing the workload and increasing the quality of the resulting proposal. Research on committees has confirmed that a group size of six to eight members results in the most efficient, compatible, and workable team. Some grant members may rotate on and off the committee, not attending all meetings. For example, the person who assembles the budget may not have to be involved in every gathering of the team. The list below identifies effective roles for a successful grants team.

▶ **Team Leader:** This highly organized person guides the team and serves as team facilitator, leader, and motivator. The leader's primary goal is to ensure that all activities occur in a timely fashion so the grant deadline is met without stressing or harassing individual team members. The leader gently reminds, prods, and asks about the work in progress so all parts of a proposal come together as planned and on time.

► **Skilled Writer:** This individual has the job of assembling all parts of the grant submitted by the different writers and editing the work to yield consistent language, proper grammar, smooth flow, clear messages, and coherence. The result should be one cohesive "piece of art" for the reviewer who is often scanning the proposal. The writer can be an English teacher, an 11th or 12th grade honor student, or a newspaper reporter with a journalism degree—someone who is a really good writer and interested in the job.

► **Budget Developer:** The team will need someone skilled in creating proposal budgets that support the program narrative. While this does not have to be an accountant, it should be someone who is not intimidated by numbers, such as a math teacher or banker.

► **Literature Researcher:** This individual can significantly contribute to the process by assessing the literature concerning the problems to be addressed in the proposal. To make a compelling case for your proposal, this person needs to be involved early on in the process. Find someone who doesn't mind spending long hours in the library or surfing the web. For example, many recent college graduates or graduate students have received training on electronic research and make good candidates for this role. In Steps 3 and 4, we'll identify the types of research you will need to conduct.

► **Program Experts:** The involvement of experts can range from attendance at one grant team meeting to participation in every assembly. These experts not only know a lot about the subject, but often have a passion for the topic. In addition, they usually have access to articles and books on the subject or know other professionals in the field who can provide input toward the creation of your grant proposal.

➤ **Needs Assessment Coordinator:** This team member is responsible for researching the statistics, conducting surveys or interviews, and seeking information that can document or prove the need and substantiate the problem. This person—an analytical thinker is best—should be trained on how to perform appropriate needs assessments, which we will explore in Step 3.

➤ **Word Processor:** Our research and experience indicate that a proposal that is pleasing to the eye will score higher. Consider administrative assistants or students with good computer skills and an attention to detail to word-process your proposal.

➤ **Community Key Informants and Consumers:** Often it is important to bring in representatives from the community as members of the grantwriting team, especially members of the target population who will be served by the grant program. Always interview representatives from the target population to learn firsthand their beliefs about the cause of the problem and how they think it should be addressed. Both brainstorming with and bouncing ideas off consumers are excellent methods to ensure that what you are proposing matches what the potential consumers perceive they need and want.

➤ **Proofreader:** This very important team member should **not** be involved in the planning and meetings because it becomes too easy to read what one thinks the proposal will say. This should be a picky person with an eye for detail and **plenty** of sleep the night before they are needed.

➤ **Gopher:** Last but **not** least, this is the person who will run errands such as picking up letters of support. Too often, one person tries to "do it all" and is running errands on the day the proposal is due rather than giving it that final polish. These minor activities distract your key contributors and damage your proposal's chances of success.

►► *Maintain group cohesiveness.*

Thoughtfully and deliberately identify members for your grants team who are talented, organized, dependable, cooperative, and especially those who have a passion for your project. Don't just look for bodies; they may attend one meeting and then never be heard from again! And don't assemble a group of "yes men" and "yes women" who will agree with you on every step, yet never truly contribute to the process.

Successful management of a grantwriting team requires attention to minimizing the natural friction created as diverse personalities work together. Your challenge will be to blend the input, efforts, and contributions from idealist and realist; bleeding heart and nay-sayer; liberal and conservative; visionary and narrow-mind; and naïve Nelly and number cruncher. One common stumbling block may be the nature of many grantwriters who prefer to work in isolation. This "Lone Ranger" approach often results in an unfunded proposal or, if funded, a project that fails when implemented.

Most proposals will benefit from the multiple viewpoints provided by a grantwriting team that adequately perceives the need and designs a comprehensive program. *As a company, we have written some exciting grant proposals that were funded but failed miserably when implemented because we did not solicit the advice and assistance of other key people and consumers.* Your grants team is critical: assemble one.

►► *Consider different types of grantwriting teams.*

There are different types of grantwriting teams. For illustrative purposes, we'll use a school district setting to exemplify team types, although the same principles apply for private nonprofits, faith-based organizations, universities, and government agencies. The following represent several viable models for constructing grantwriting teams:

► **Classroom- or Discipline-Based Team:** Within a single school, a group of teachers from one or several similar disciplines (i.e., music, art, dance, and drama) might assemble a team to develop grants in the areas of their training, education, interest, and experience. There could also be multidisciplinary teams within the school that would focus on smaller grants ($500 to $25,000) that have a single focus.

➤ **School-Based Team:** The school should develop an interdisciplinary team consisting of members from a cross section of disciplines. This school-wide team would write grant proposals that address the needs of the school as a whole, usually through larger grants. Grants of this nature often have multiple program components that combine to form a single proposal in the medium range of $25,000 to $100,000. For example, an afterschool program could consist of technology-based activities, recreation, cultural enrichment, homework assistance, transportation, and counseling components.

➤ **School District Team:** Selected members from the school-based grantwriting teams, joined by district personnel, may form a district team that would focus on the largest, multi-component grants (usually greater than $100,000).

➤ **Interagency Team:** Members from the district team (or district personnel) can join with local, private nonprofit programs, government agencies, and civic organizations to form a collaborative partnership for the submission of large grant proposals, $100,000 and above. Requests for Proposals (RFPs) from funding sources are distributed to a wide range of local agencies, and it is important to form alliances with other community agencies for this and other reasons. Through an interagency team, one agency serves as the lead fiscal agent on behalf of the partnership, the team develops the proposal and shares the work, and grant funds are distributed among participating agencies once the grant is funded. Too often, agencies are unwilling to collaborate or share grant monies; as a result, they miss out on many funding opportunities. With nearly every funding source emphasizing and rewarding partnerships, agencies that do collaborate will score higher and enhance their likelihood of success. A collaborative interagency grantwriting team sets the stage for this winning scenario!

▶▶ *Train and support the team.*

It is critical that all team members receive grants development training because intimidation is the number one killer of successful grant teams. Every member needs professional training on how to find and write grants, and everyone needs a working knowledge of how to assemble grants in the most logical way and in the least amount of time. Organizations should invest in quality training. Apply the adage, "It takes money to make money." Make the investment in grants development training for your team from a variety of companies and organizations; it will pay rich dividends.

The agency should commit to providing grantwriters with a supportive environment for grantwriting. Environmental support ranges from ensuring adequate workspace and sufficient technology to freedom from distractions and flexible work schedules to providing creature comforts such as snacks, especially near grant deadlines.

The organization must also recognize that people work more efficiently and effectively if they are rewarded for their work. Organizational reinforcement of team efforts can include bonuses, extra time off, funding for travel to national conferences, extra equipment, and consulting work. Above all, recognize team members in front of their peers and the community when they are successful. And remember, not all of their efforts will be successful. *Some of the best grants written by Research Associates were not funded due to reasons beyond our control.* Grants team members will perform consistently better with encouragement, support, and motivation.

Avoiding Pitfalls

We've Been There, Done That!

At Research Associates, our professional grants development team recently developed six state government grants that focused on adult literacy, reading, and early childhood education totaling nearly $4 million in potential funding. Although we managed to produce some really nice proposals for our customers, we made numerous mistakes. It is important to continually examine the processes within your organizations and agencies to assess weaknesses and refine the internal grants development process.

The situations below illustrate the types of errors even a professional firm can commit. We hope that you will learn from our mistakes, which inspired **The Murphy DuBose Grantwriting Laws.**

➤ **The more experience you have, the more you learn you're not an expert on everything.** *The project was beyond our expertise.* These grants were based upon scientific research that was complex and difficult to understand; we were in over our heads. We should have reviewed the Request for Proposals more carefully before accepting this assignment and consulted a reading expert. We also should have considered our current workload. Yes, greed captured us, hook, line, and sinker!

➤ **When writing a grant, different versions of the RFP will find their way into your office.** *We had two versions of the RFP.* A couple of weeks into the grants development process, we realized that one writer was using an older version of the grant application that had been distributed at the Bidders' Conference. This could have been disastrous.

➤ **Two word-processing software programs are not better than one.** *We didn't coordinate our software programs.* Different writers were using different software programs. While documents can be moved between Word and WordPerfect, transfers result in format and possibly other changes. We should have used one program.

➤ **The more important the deadline, the more often it is missed.** *We didn't establish realistic deadlines.* We allowed clients to have input into the proposal until the final day. We should have established an earlier cutoff date and time for accepting comments from customers. Our continued, last- minute revisions nearly resulted in our missing the application deadline—not to mention we were forced to seriously exceed the speed limit to deliver the proposals on time!

➤ **When the pressure is greatest, interruptions will increase.** *We weren't focused as the deadline approached.* We allowed other distractions such as answering telephones on the day the grant was due, when we should have relied on caller ID to screen callers during the final hours. One of our more "challenging" clients called the vice president of our Grants Division the morning of the grant deadline. Neglecting to check caller ID before answering the phone, she learned, to her dismay, this extremely demanding client was on the other end of the line! The caller was using a speakerphone with mild static and asked, "Can you hear me?" With the quick thinking inspired only by sheer panic, she replied: "Hello! Hello! Are you there? I can't hear you!" and quickly hung up the phone!

➤ **The larger the team, the more you will hear, "I thought you told them."** *We didn't coordinate or communicate well within the team.* Each writer "helped" by making copies of the appendices before coming to the central office for final proposal assembly. When grantwriters and proposals arrived with only limited time remaining, we frantically tried to assemble the proposal components. With our high fatigue levels on that final day, even a minor task proved difficult. It would have been much easier to bring one set of appendices and run collated copies at the main office.

➤ **The closer the finish line, the more vague the directions.** *We did not check the address of the funding source carefully.* The grants division of the state department had moved. Although this was clearly documented in the grant application, with only minutes until the deadline, we were in the wrong building, desperately seeking new directions for proposal delivery!

➤ **A proofreader is never around when you need one.** *We did not plan for final editing.* By the final hours, the attention level of our grantwriters had dropped significantly. Unfortunately, we failed to have a fresh technical writer available to make a final review of the entire document, which would have avoided a few minor glitches. (We now have four technical writers on retainer.)

➤ **The more you want something specific from employees, the less they read your mind.** *We had woefully inadequate communications between the grantwriters and technical writer.* In our rush, we e-mailed the narrative to a technical writer, instructing her to "proof the final document." What we wanted was a review of the document for any typographical or grammatical errors. What happened was that parts of the narrative were rewritten, deleting some critical emotional language and lessening the impact of the text. Sadly, there was not time to reinsert the vivid, emotional language that had been struck. (Thankfully, the proposal was funded.)

➤ **In any crisis, your most reliable person will have a dead cell phone.** In our rush out of the door, we left one important document behind. We realized this as we were approaching the delivery point, but the main office was closed. The first staff member we tried to call had a "dead" cell phone. A second staffer had a cell phone but neglected to turn it on! Thank goodness, we reached another staff person who raced to the office and retrieved the missing document.

The Murphy DuBose Grantwriting Laws definitely created unnecessary stress for our grants team during this near fiasco. These are the kinds of problems a carefully planned process and a coordinated team effort will avoid.

In Closing: Now that agency processes are in place, we will turn our attention to Step 2, and tell you how to locate grants. *There are billions of dollars out there!*

STEP 2
FINDING FUNDING
SOURCES

One of our former workshop participants wrote a one-page letter to the Delta Airlines Foundation and received a $5,000 grant to establish a recreation program. A group of elementary school teachers who attended our training wrote a three-page concept paper and received $50,000 from McDonald Douglas Corporation to establish a technology lab at their school with computer hardware and software as well as digital and video cameras. By submitting a two-page concept paper, a third participant received a $500,000 grant from the General Electric Foundation for assisting high-poverty students with attending college!

These attendees said that before they received training about finding and writing grants, they simply did not know the tremendous number of resources available. Now, they're going after millions!

Our research indicates that more than 60,000 foundations, 5,000 corporations, and thousands of government programs currently support a wide variety of grant programs. In fact, sources indicate there will be over $450 billion in funding awarded during 2005. But if you can't find the source, you can't ask for the money. Let's take a look at where you can find the money.

Foundation, Corporate, and Government Grants

Show Us the Money!

Before getting into specific funding resources, we have an important piece of advice: As you seek funding sources, think creatively. If you cannot meet all your needs with one grant, consider going after several smaller grants that could add up to the support you need. Also, one of the current trends is that many funding sources prefer to award grants to partnerships or collaborations of multiple agencies. While your agency may not be eligible to apply for a specific grant, you can partner with other organizations that may then subcontract with your agency to provide the services, allocating part of the funds to your agency. Fore example, each year there are state drug enforcement grants available to city or county government agencies through the state public safety agency. Though it seems that schools are not eligible for these funds, they can partner with city or county law enforcement and apply to fund a DARE (Drug Awareness Resistance Education) officer for their school.

▶▶ *Sources for Grant Programs*

There are several types of grant programs from various sources that require very specific approaches. For this reason, the most successful grants development programs build a diversified resource development strategy, seeking grants from several sources and never relying on any one type of funding to support their cause. The various resources are discussed below.

▶   **Federal Government Grant Programs:** Federal grants are the most complex, competitive, and lengthy. However, they typically offer larger awards, fund for multiple years, and more recently, have actually reduced the administrative burden, or "strings," traditionally attached to these grants. Federal grants are announced in the *Federal Register,* which is published daily. Although subscriptions cost more than $800 annually, this information is available on the Internet at **www.gpoaccess.gov/fr**. Government agencies list their grant programs and other news in the *Federal Register.* Since November 2003, all federal grant opportunities are posted at **www.grants.gov**. Most federal grants are announced early in the federal fiscal year, between November and March. In the table of contents or index of an issue, scan for "grants availability." The law requires that federal agencies announce their programs for public input prior to the official notification of grant availability, giving prospective applicants a sneak peek at what is to come. By identifying grants in the fall or early winter, grantseekers will have several months to prepare for the grant process—much better than the standard 45 to 60 days after the grant is formally announced in late winter or spring.

➤ **State Government Grant Funds:** State government grants are easier to write than their federal counterparts, but they often distribute smaller awards limited to one-year funding *(state-level distribution of federal funds is often multiyear)*. On average, state governments offer about 60 different grant programs. However, state government grants are spread among many agencies and can be difficult to locate since most states do not have a central grants-announcement mechanism. One key to finding these grants is to obtain a copy of your state government telephone directory, available from larger magazine stores. Next, contact a mid-level manager in an appropriate division of the state agency to inquire about the availability of grants. For example, to review technology grants for schools, call someone in the technology division at your state department of education. Another route is to use an Internet search engine and simply type in a specific state agency or your state's name to link to relevant government agencies. Most state agency website list grant opportunities.

➤ **City and County Government Grants:** Local governments receive monies through block grants such as the Community Development Block Grant Program (CDBG) and from local taxes. These grants are based upon needs identified by public hearings and are coordinated through the economic and planning divisions within city and county governments. While often politically sensitive, local grants fund a wide variety of programs. Local grants such as beautification grants and accommodations tax grants for special events can be perfect opportunities for nonprofits to partner with a city agency. Local grants are typically smaller than federal and state government programs and are usually allocated on an annual basis.

➤ **Foundation Funding:** There are more than 60,000 national, state, regional, and local foundations that fund a wide variety of grant proposals. Foundations are generally interested in the well-being of communities and often seek projects that test new strategies and share information with other organizations (so others benefit from learning what worked and did not work in a program). Foundations vary in requirements, but most require a limited amount of information making proposals short in length. Many foundations, even those such as the Kellogg Foundation with billions of dollars in assets, accept online applications. Other foundations, such as the Ford Foundation which also has billions in the bank, allocate thousands of grants each year and will respond to your proposal in 30 days or less. You can learn about foundations by checking grant directories or in the reference section of large libraries. Internet search engines, also yield much information on "foundation grants."

➤ **Corporate Grants:** There are thousands of corporations that allocate grants. The average funding level for a corporate grant is around $50,000, but corporations have a different focus. They are interested in promoting their products, increasing profits, assisting employees and their families, creating public awareness, and enhancing tax write-offs. In discussions with our company, the vice president of an automobile manufacturer remarked, "Like many companies today, we plan to invest our grant dollars into programs that improve the quality of employees available to us, such as using technology in the workplace." Consequently, when you write a corporate grant proposal, you must focus not only on your needs, but also on how your project will promote or help the corporation.

In addition, most large companies have both a corporate giving program and a national or regional foundation. For example, the BellSouth Corporation provides grants through corporate giving and also maintains the BellSouth Foundation that focuses on education and technology. You should obtain a corporate foundation directory and also visit your local Chamber of Commerce for a listing of the Fortune 500 businesses in your community. Chances are your corporate neighbor also has a foundation that distributes millions of dollars annually. Keep in mind, however, that you should start with your local company manager before heading to the corporate office.

►► *Guidelines for Finding Grants*

In our grants development training sessions, we've heard many times that successful grantwriters invest sufficient funds to compile the resources needed to find grants. We recommend six avenues for finding grants and developing resources.

► **Directories:** Obtain grant directories that pinpoint the best grant programs or the "cream of the crop" in funding sources. These grant directories can be highly specialized publications (such as funding for technology) or can have a broader focus (such as the largest national foundations that fund many types of programs). Most large libraries carry grant directories, but many are voluminous and outdated. Look for private companies that update their directories once or twice a year for the latest information about funding opportunities. (Research Associates publishes over 50 different grant directories.)

► **Newsletters:** Subscribe to a grants newsletter that provides up-to-date information about existing and new grant programs. Go to any Internet search engine and type in "grants newsletter" for a listing of publications. (Research Associates publishes a grants newsletter that identifies over 1,000 grants annually.)

► **The Internet:** Take advantage of the power of the Internet, an invaluable resource for grantwriters. Most funding sources and their website provide detailed information about their grant programs and offer helpful explanations about the application process.

► **Grants Development Training:** Obtain the grants development training you need by attending grant seminars and conferences that offer certification in the field. Find one that gives you hands-on, practical lessons. For example, in our most recent grants development workshop, various work groups, organized by discipline, learned how to write grants. At the same time, this format facilitated some great networking and the exchange of resources. Identify several companies that provide training and participate in a number of different trainings. Gaining perspectives from different companies will help you develop your grantwriting theory and methodology into a fine art. Be sure to research the firm's track record and ask for references when assessing potential training. (For information about Research Associates certified grants development courses, visit our website at **www.grantexperts.com**. Other quality training programs include offerings from The Foundation Center, **www.fdncenter.org**, and the Grantmanship Center, **www.tgci.com**).

► **Professional Associations:** Your professional associations that have staff at the state or national level will often know about grants or foundations that have supported comparable groups in other locations. Also check your professional publications for articles and announcements about company support for organizations in other locales.

► **Collaboration:** Finally, let everyone in your community know you are a grantwriter interested in collaboration with other agencies. Grant programs are announced in countless ways and contact with professionals in other disciplines is every writer's best asset.

Understanding the Request for Proposals (RFP)

What Do Funders Want to Buy?

In this section, we describe the initial steps in our model grantwriting process—those that involve obtaining, analyzing, and applying grant application guidelines.

Grant application guidelines are usually issued in a document called the Request for Proposals (RFP), although they are also known as the Request for Applications (RFA) or the Notice of Funding Availability (NOFA). Funding sources differ in their methods for soliciting grant-related information, and consequently, their application guidelines vary. Some funders request a simple one-page letter, while others require the completion of a short application form. Many larger funding sources explain their application process in a complex, highly detailed RFP that may be 30 to 75 pages in length.

A comprehensive RFP reveals the "heart" or intention of the funding source by describing the populations and problems they want to impact through their assistance. Thus, analyzing the RFP is the key to beginning a successful grantwriting process, since it provides a road map or guide to the type of program the funding source will fund. While some RFPs are very clear, sufficiently detailed, and well organized, others may appear to be written by someone who has never read or written a grant proposal or guidelines! Regardless of the application's format, you will enhance your chances of success by adhering to these two rules:

1. **Obtain the grant application and guidelines as early as possible.** Obviously, the more time you are given to consider an application and develop a proposal, the more favorable your chances of success. Unfortunately, the application may be distributed to a number of locations including the desks of community leaders, universities, private nonprofits, government agencies, and school districts. Typically, the application is circulated among a variety of parties, consuming valuable development time before it eventually lands on the grantwriter's

desk, perhaps only days from the application deadline. Establishing a workable grants development process (explained in Step 1) can minimize these unfortunate delays.

2. **Follow all application guidelines.** After reviewing thousands of RFPs and grant proposals, we have found the most common error made by grantwriters is their failure to examine and follow the application guidelines precisely. Successful grantwriters adopt and apply specific tactics to satisfy the requirements of RFPs. The   steps that follow describe our model methodology.

▶▶ *Keep the original grant application.*

When you receive the grant application, make two clean copies of the RFP. Store the original in a manila folder created for the grant. Use the other copy as a master for making additional copies to use or distribute as needed during the proposal's development. As you review the copied RFP, make notes on it and highlight key points.

If you received the grant application electronically (i.e., downloaded from the funder's website), save the file on your hard drive and on a diskette, zip disk, or CD. (We prefer the zip disk since it can store all of the many files created for the grant.) Place the storage medium containing the application and a printed version of the application in a manila folder. This step may seem inconsequential, but repeatedly we have had to return to this file to retrieve a clean copy of a required form or specific RFP information.

Further, the original RFP is considered the basis of the contract between the funding agency and the applicant. Therefore, you may need the original RFP after the program has been completed during final evaluation, reporting, and the required audits of grant funds.

▶▶ *Decide if you should apply for the grant.*

During the grant preparation process, you must thoroughly review every aspect of the RFP. Initially, your foremost concern is whether or not you should apply for the grant. (You will not yet be concerned with details about format, layout, program content, or budget requirements.) With a highlighting pen in hand, carefully review the RFP to determine the feasibility of applying for the funding. Consider these issues and ask these questions as you read:

► **Eligibility:** Is our agency or one of our partners eligible to apply for this grant? Does the funding source provide grants in our geographical area? Will any of the application's restrictions impact our decision to apply?

► **Time Frame:** When is the grant due? Do we have time to apply for this proposal considering our current and projected workloads and personal commitments?

► **Effort Required:** How much work is involved? Do we have the resources to construct the grant by the deadline? What is the grant's maximum page length? Do we have the required expertise to draft a successful model or can we consult with someone who does?

► **Appropriateness:** Do our organization's mission, program activities, and financial needs correspond with the grant program's goals and requirements? *Don't make the mistake of chasing dollars that will not support your mission!*

► **Return on Investment:** What is the amount of grant funding allowed? Is that amount worth the work required by the RFP?

► **Likelihood for Success:** How many grants will be awarded? How many organizations are likely to apply? *These are key factors in assessing success potential.*

Each of these issues must be analyzed carefully since they will impact your potential for success. If the grant development team or key decision makers believe the organization's chances of receiving the funding are less than 50 percent, you may decide to discontinue your pursuit of the grant. When this happens, consider forwarding the application to another agency partner or grantwriter who has more time available. Many grantwriters experience low success rates (and burn out) because they apply for every grant they can find. Some of these grant programs do not fit the organization's strategic plan or mission, or the grantwriters may not have sufficient time or resources to develop an appropriate proposal. A feasibility review will help the applying organization avoid this pitfall.

During the initial RFP review, keep in mind that perception can be influenced by disposition, alertness, workloads, stress, and fluctuating energy levels. For this reason, plan to review the RFP repeatedly—on various days and at different times of day. (It is surprising how differently an RFP is perceived each time it is examined.) Use multicolored highlighting pens to emphasize differing areas as you review the RFP. This will help organize the information provided in the application. To ensure that we understand every aspect of the application at Research Associates, we typically review the RFP numerous times before finally deciding to pursue a grant.

▶▶ *Determine what the funding source wants.*

Many grant proposals fail because the mission and goals of the proposed program do not mirror the guidelines and intentions of the funding source. Most RFPs suggest specific program activities, strategies, and services they seek to fund. Also, RFPs often provide current research references and literature sources to consider when describing program components. Some funding sources provide previously funded grants (or post them on their website) to provide applicants with sample programs and successful projects in the field.

Grantwriters should develop a one-page overview of the RFP that highlights its goals, the main purpose of the grant, acceptable budget expenses, and allowable program activities. This summary will facilitate the decision-making of busy key players (such as project managers, community partners, and grant team members) by providing a succinct outline of the program. Research Associates has successfully applied this methodology in helping our customers to understand the proposal and follow the funding source's guidelines. This overview is also helpful for collaborative community partners who may be asked to write a letter of support and commitment for your program.

Think of the RFP as an advertisement explaining what the funding source wants to buy. As grantwriters, we must prepare an attractive, sellable product that also satisfies our customers, clients, and colleagues. Ideally, an agency should conduct an internal needs assessment of the issues it wants to address (and the related financial requirements) before considering grant applications. Then, when an RFP is reviewed, the organization can compare its identified needs with the grant application's intentions to measure its potential for funding success. The successful grantwriter will match the RFP requirements with local needs, the literature, and pre-existing model program activities that are already nationally successful (often called "best practices"). In working with clients, Research Associates develops an interview form based upon these four components to help guide and educate customers about the grant program while enhancing the success of their proposal. Consequently, local customers and community partners are able to integrate the program activities and budget items they want, but their choices are limited to the RFP allowances and the literature.

▶▶ *Format the proposal as described in the RFP.*

The RFP usually specifies formatting requirements and provides required forms. If you decide to pursue this grant funding, you will need to keep these requirements in mind as you develop and draft your proposal. Review the RFP to ascertain formatting guidelines such as the following:

► **Pages:** Is the total number of pages or pages per section limited in the proposal? Do the page numbers need to be formatted a certain way (e.g., centered)?

► **Arrangement and Formatting of Sections:** Does the wording of the RFP suggest certain titles for section headings and subheadings (e.g., major areas to be addressed)? Is a grant review form included, which may be used in grading the proposal? Does the RFP provide a specific outline to be followed? The grantwriter should utilize these guidelines appropriately since reviewers will usually grade the proposal according to these same questions or subheadings, and often in the order in which they are presented in the RFP.

➤ **Formatting Specifics:** Does the RFP provide formatting specifics, such as font size (e.g., 12 point), font type (e.g., Times New Roman), word limitations, line spacing (e.g., single or double), and margin size (e.g., one inch)? *To minimize problems, distribute these details to all grants development team members so everyone uses the same format while creating proposal components. Or better yet, create a document template that is distributed to all contributors.*

➤ **Appendices**: Can appendices be included? Are there required items or exclusions from the appendices?

RA Note: If your RFP does not address these issues, Research Associates' recommendations are included at appropriate points throughout our 12 steps of grants development.

▶▶ *Submit questions to the funding source.*

During your initial analysis of the RFP, you may think of questions the RFP does not answer. These might include, for example, issues regarding your eligibility-to-apply status or the scope of allowable program activities. Most RFPs will include the name and contact information for the person who oversees the application process. Before you contact them, we strongly recommend that you assemble a list of **all** of your questions so you can address these issues in one call (to avoid being labeled as a problem or pesky applicant). When you do call, consider asking if they will share copies of previously funded grant proposals; you will be surprised how often this resource is available, but only if you ask.

▶▶ *Attend the applicantsí workshop (or bidders' conference).*

As part of the grant application process, many funding sources offer a technical assistance workshop or bidders' conference about the grant program during which an overview is presented and questions are addressed. If several sessions are being held, we recommend that you attend the last scheduled workshop. By that time, the representatives from the funding source will have heard a wide range of questions and will probably be better prepared to answer questions and address issues that arise. These workshops are important because you will often hear helpful clarifications about topics not covered in the RFP. This information gives the grantwriter an advantage and potential access to important issues that would otherwise have remained inaccessible (e.g., learning about the latest research and model programs). Be sure to sign in and provide your e-mail and mailing address to the sponsor, since additional information is often distributed to registered attendees.

►► *Review the RFP one more time.*

Near the end of your proposal development (in Steps 10 or 11) as your draft enters the final stages, ask several individuals with various backgrounds, expertise levels, and experience to read the RFP and your proposal one final time to ensure you have covered all of the details. More than likely, they will find a few items that were omitted. These details may seem small, but they could make a difference in the points you receive, and this could determine your success or failure. Do you see why the best grantwriters are sometimes considered obsessive, compulsive, neurotic perfectionists?

►► *Prepare for document submission.*

Develop a checklist covering the specifics of delivering your grant proposal to the funding source. (Steps 10 and 11 will address proposal preparation and delivery in much more detail.) Review the RFP for the details below and keep them in mind throughout grants development and deadline planning.

► **Due Date:** When is the proposal due? Does it need to be physically delivered to the funding source by that date, or will a postmark by the U.S. Postal Service suffice? Can we use commercial carriers such as UPS or Federal Express? Does the due date fall on a weekend or holiday, and if so, will the proposal be due the following workday?

► **Address:** Where should the document be sent? What is the mailing address? Are mailed documents and commercially delivered packages sent to the same or different addresses? Be careful—even zip codes may vary according to delivery method.

► **Number of Copies:** How many copies and originals must be sent?

► **Final Product:** How should the proposal be assembled (i.e., clipped, stapled, with rubber bands, etc.)? If stapling is preferred, should it be fastened in a specific location (e.g., the upper left corner)?

► **Packaging:** Do we have the supplies needed to send this package (e.g., the correct size of shipping box)?

► **Identification:** Do we know the specific name of the grant program, so it can be written on the outside of the shipping box for identification by the funding source? (Some federal grant programs require that you include the Catalog of Federal Domestic Assistance, or CFDA number.) What is the telephone number of the funding source (a requirement of commercial carriers)?

In Closing: Throughout Step 2, we established the components of a model grantwriting process that address finding grants and analyzing application requirements. Our next chapter will focus on developing the Problem or Need Statement of your grant proposal. The successful grantwriter must know how to document the reasons their community (and thus, their organization) needs the grant funds more than any other applicant. We'll show you how.

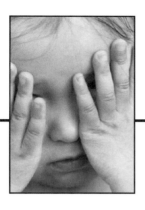

STEP 3
DEFINING THE
PROBLEM

The first section of the program narrative in most grant proposals is generally the section that identifies the problem or problems in the target population that your program will address. This section is called the **Problem Statement** or, sometimes, the **Needs Statement**.

In our grants development workshops, we often state that our goal in writing the Problem Statement is "to make the reviewer cry." This is because we believe the key to developing a successful grant application lies in describing a compelling need in your community or target population. There are several points to keep in mind as you define and delineate the problems your proposed program will address.

▶▶ *Assume readers know nothing about your community.*

Write your Problem Statement as if the reader knows absolutely nothing about your state, your county, your community, or your target population. You must clearly describe every aspect of your community relevant to the proposal.

For example, we know that our home state, South Carolina, consistently ranks poorly in many quality-of-life statistics. Our population is extremely poor, and most of our counties are isolated and rural. Yet, we may have a federal grants reviewer from Ohio whose experience with South Carolina is limited to vacations at an exclusive coastal resort near the city of Charleston. Despite the reviewer's sense of familiarity with our state, the devastating poverty and isolation choking our small rural counties must be clearly defined or this reviewer will fail to and appropriately perceive our urgent need for assistance.

▶▶ *Assume readers are unfamiliar with your problems.*

Keep in mind that the reader may be unaware of the relationships between appalling demographics, underlying causes, and resulting problems. For this reason, you should use caution and clearly explain these relationships when they are applicable.

If you cite, for example, the high incidence of single-parent families in a community as evidence of need, you may, in fact, anger a reviewer who is a single parent. Thus, if you choose to use this demographic, you must explain its relationship to other factors that you are planning to address (e.g., higher poverty levels, lower parental involvement in health issues, or higher numbers of unsupervised children in the community).

Also keep in mind that the reviewer may not be familiar with the national and state averages for statistics that you employ. For this reason, you should always "set the stage" for your descriptive statistics by comparing national and/or state data and rankings to those of your target population. This will provide the reviewer perspective for your community statistics and help the reader evaluate the severity of your need. For a state proposal, compare the state to both your county and community. It can also be illuminating to use rankings for these comparisons, e.g., "South Carolina is the 49th worst in high school graduation rates (United Health Rankings, 2004)." In a federal government or national foundation proposal, compare the national statistics to your state data and then to your county and/or community information.

For example, in a federal application targeting schools serving high numbers of low-income families, we employed a common education standard for poverty: the number of students qualifying for free and reduced-cost lunch. Our description offered national and state comparisons:

In South Carolina, a state ranked nearly last in almost every economic indicator, our four counties represent the poorest of the poor. For example, 40% of students nationally qualify for free or reduced-cost lunch, while in South Carolina, nearly 50% of students qualify. In our target rural counties, a staggering 92% are eligible for this benefit.

RA Tip! If you choose to employ county rankings in a national application, always state the number of counties so the reviewer can interpret your ranking. For example, "Sample County ranks 44th highest out of 46 South Carolina counties in the percentage of children living below poverty (US Census 2000)."

▶▶ *Solicit input from different sectors.*

Always examine community needs and problems from as many perspectives as possible. Every individual offers unique insights based on personal experience, education, upbringing, family history, age, sex, race, culture, and a host of additional factors. Use this input to broaden your own interpretation of community problems. As a grants developer, you can design effective programs and services only after you understand every possible aspect of the problem.

Several years ago, we were asked to help develop a grant program targeting adolescent, minority, unwed mothers with multiple unmet needs. This population was slipping through the cracks of traditional healthcare, the educational system, and established family support services. A program was desperately needed, and a number of community stakeholders had come together in an effort to assess and address the problem. When we arrived, the planning task force had gathered to review the situation and make recommendations.

As we entered the room, we knew immediately our planning efforts were in trouble—every member of the task force was middle-aged, Caucasian, and male. How could this group comprehend the needs of the target population?

▶▶ *Think negatively as you describe your community problems.*

Your goal as a grantwriter is to compel the reviewer to want to help your community by funding your program. You should employ strong language to depict the worst aspects of life for your target population. The Problem Statement is not the setting for descriptions of anything positive that may be happening in your community (this will come later in the Approach section). The Problem Statement should describe only the worst aspects of your community.

RA Secret! Occasionally you will unexpectedly encounter favorable statistics. When this occurs, you may need to research more deeply because these statistics may be misleading. Ferreting out the cause of a surprisingly positive statistic may also reveal additional community needs. For example, in a county with extremely high rates of poverty, we discovered the unemployment rate had unexpectedly improved during the last two years. Additional research and interviews with local key informants revealed the underlying cause of the employment number. We included the statistic along with its disturbingly negative implications as follows:

> Surprisingly, the unemployment rate has recently improved to the state average, but this trend is misleading as it does not reflect local jobs. These "statistics" are the young mothers who climb onto buses before dawn every morning for the ride to minimum wage jobs at a coastal resort, not returning until 7 or 8 each night.

Conducting the Needs Assessment

Digging for the Dirt!

Independent, reliable assessment of the needs in your community is necessary to validate your observations and conclusions about community problems. There are many avenues available, and the successful grantwriter employs several methods of assessing need and documenting community problems. In writing the grant proposal, your goal is to convince the reader the needs in your community are not only greater than everyone else's but are also the most compelling.

A successful proposal should include at least four or five different types of credible, independent documentation of community needs. As you gather and review data from different sources, select those statistics that portray your needs in the most persuasive manner. All cited statistics should be referenced by source and date. It is also preferable that no data cited be more than three years old.

Also be aware that if the data available from the most recent year is a marked improvement after several consistent years of more dismal figures, then it may be an outlier, that is, a statistic heavily influenced by fluctuation or natural variance. In other words, it may not be reliable. For this reason, you may elect to employ a statistic that is slightly older if it more accurately reflects the problem that you are addressing. To ensure accuracy, examine data over several years.

Here are ten methods of assessing community need that offer a broad range of practical approaches to this task.

(1) Research available statistics.

Statistics are readily available to the diligent researcher. The U.S. Census Bureau offers a variety of statistics at the national, state, county, and census-tract levels. (Census tracts are the smallest geographic areas for which census data is available.)

In addition, every state has a state census data center that can provide customized statistics upon request. For a relatively small investment, you may gain invaluable information for the target populations your agency serves. This is done by taking a detailed county or city map, drawing lines around a particular neighborhood (your target area), and submitting this map to the state census data center. Then for a fee (probably $200 or less), the center will provide census statistics for the target neighborhood.

CENSUS BUREAU WEBSITES

US Census Bureau
www.census.gov

State and County Quick Facts
http://quickfacts.census.gov/qfd

Census Tract Locator
www.census.gov/geo/www/tract.html

For example, we were assisting a community agency serving a South Carolina county that—sadly for the grantwriters—was a relatively affluent. (The county ranked second highest in average income.) However, the agency was not targeting the entire county; it was focused on serving several inner-city neighborhoods with high-risk families and rampant poverty. Therefore, we sought more targeted statistics using census tracts from the state census data center. The plight of these neighborhoods became obvious with the more targeted data. At the county level, the appalling statistics for the high-risk neighborhoods had been masked by the affluence of the suburbs, but the detailed maps revealed clear areas of need.

The Internet offers numerous sources for state and county statistics. If you are unsure how to begin an Internet search, go to a search engine such as those available at **www.yahoo.com, www.google.com,** or **www.excite.com**. By simply entering your state's name and the word "statistics" in the search box, you will access a wealth of linked information on almost any topic you can imagine.

For example, a recent search at www.yahoo.com for "South Carolina Statistics" yielded 61 sites. The first selection was "SCIway," the "South Carolina Information Highway" site of South Carolina Statistics and Statistical Reports. This site offers links to (1) SC Statistical Abstracts; (2) Area Statistics and Rankings by place, city, county, state, and congressional district; (3) Kids Count by state, county, county ranking, topic, and trends; (4) U.S. Census information in five formats; and (5) Statistics by Topic including agriculture, forestry, fishing, mining; banking and finance; business; climate and geography; crime and criminal justice; economics; education; elections; employment; energy resources; government and politics; health and public welfare; housing; income; population; recreation, travel, and tourism; transportation; and vital statistics.

RA Tip! Among our favorite sources for county and state statistics are the Kids Count national data compilations on the well-being of children provided by the Annie E. Casey Foundation. You may access this information online at **www.aecf.org/kidscount/census**. While most states are accessible through this website, always consult individual state statistical directories for more detailed state and local data.

(2) Conduct surveys.

Sometimes a simple survey conducted in the target area will provide insightful, useful information. This can be helpful when there are no statistics readily available for the target population and time or monetary constraints do not permit a customized state census data report. It is advisable to employ standard sampling practices by making sure your sample is drawn randomly from the target population and honestly represents the larger population you are describing.

Because many of Research Associates' clients are schools and school districts, we are often challenged to document the need of a target population whose children attend a certain elementary school. The principal may "know" this student population is poorer than either the county at large or the school district (for which statistics are available). Yet, this observation—even from an informed professional—is anecdotal at best and insufficient for documenting need. Here are two examples of how Research Associates surveyed target areas:

➤ In one instance, we prepared a simple six-question survey written on a fifth-grade reading level with questions about housing, available transportation, and employment. At this particular school, administrators had done an excellent job of engaging faculty in the grants development process, and teachers were very supportive of our survey efforts. They encouraged students to bring back completed, signed surveys with candy rewards. Thanks to this enthusiastic faculty support, within three days we had an 88 percent response rate. We were then able to compute some simple demographics and cite this "recent school survey" in the Problem Statement of our grant proposal.

➤ In another community, we conducted a door-to-door survey in a target neighborhood. We used graduate students in social work who were experienced in interviewing individuals from a variety of cultural and ethnic backgrounds. We designed a short, simply worded questionnaire and then developed an engaging description of our role in trying to get money for needed services at the local elementary school. We obtained donations of $5 gift coupons from a nearby grocery store and offered these coupons as incentives to every head of household willing to participate in our brief interview. In one day, we managed to survey slightly more than half of the target population, providing our planners with valuable insights and information.

(3) Hold community meetings.

Community meetings can be a dynamic source of insights into community problems as well as an effective resource for creative, workable solutions. In addition, energetic and motivated individuals often emerge who can provide committed volunteer manpower to the grants planning process and/or the grants program advisory task force. While these meetings may sometimes be difficult to manage as different agendas are pursued, they provide the opportunity to interact with a (usually) diverse group who cares about the community and can provide important information and, occasionally, compelling quotes.

For example, while facilitating a community meeting at an elementary school, we asked an eight-year-old what he wanted to do when he grew up. His heartbreaking answer: "I want to go to jail, just like my daddy." This response strengthened the impact of our proposal, which was funded.

(4) Solicit input from the target population.

An often-overlooked source of information about any target population is the population itself. We have already discussed sampling via written surveys or interviews. Sometimes, however, simply bringing together a representative group from the impacted population to participate as a focus group can be very revealing. This process may be very structured with a series of predetermined questions, or it may be informal with a trained facilitator subtly interviewing the group to pursue shared perceptions of problems. An added benefit of focus groups is the input regarding potential and often creative solutions to community problems.

Research Associates has been rewarded with eye-opening insights during focus group interviews with a target population. These have come during both formal interviews and informal conversations with participants. For example, when developing a program to reduce dropout rates in one school district, we interviewed a group of former students who had dropped out of the school system. When asked why they thought so many students failed to graduate, they responded that it was because most students were black and most teachers were white. This comment was very helpful to school administrators who had previously failed to recognize or acknowledge the impact of this racial imbalance.

(5) Review existing studies.

Government, public, and private entities regularly perform studies and surveys in almost every community. These statistics, summaries, and recommendations can be most helpful during grants development, and (pardon the cliché) there is no reason to reinvent the wheel. We strongly recommend that you invest the time to locate and contact these "statistics keepers" in your community.

Existing sources for local statistics may include:

► **Government Entities:** Chambers of Commerce, city or county economic development boards, city or county planning departments, regional transit authorities, and local law enforcement agencies

> ► **Public Service Providers:** Health departments, mental health agencies, substance abuse prevention or treatment agencies, and community action agencies

> ► **Educational Institutions:** School districts, technical schools, and local colleges

Developing relationships with these local entities will be time well spent. Call them, make appointments, and go and meet with them. Learn what resources they offer, and let them know you are interested in their information. Explain how, as a grantwriter, you can translate their recommendations into grants dollars for the community. This will enhance your ability to develop a successful Problem Statement in a timely and efficient manner.

(6) Interview key informants in the community.

Interviews with key informants in the local community can help identify local problems. Uncovering networks among the business community and local faith-based organizations provides another excellent resource for a community needs assessment as these people possess a comprehension of local need that will enrich your understanding of the community.

Key informants can also be instrumental in approaching the community when you are seeking support for a proposed grant program. This community support is important not only during grants development, but can be critical during the review process (the role of politics will be addressed in Step 12) as well as during program implementation. The bottom line: Always identify local key informants, meet with them, listen to their input about the community, and seek their support.

(7) Interview professionals who work with the target population.

Local professionals who are familiar with the needs of the target population can also offer helpful insights for the grants development process. These professionals often have access to information unavailable by other means and can offer evidence to substantiate the severity of need in the community. Observations and quotes from medical, legal, education, and family-support professionals can provide credible evidence of community needs, corroborating hypotheses offered by proposal writers. Of course, these quotes are even more powerful when they are consistent with and supported by statistics from independent sources.

(8) Seek input from your professional colleagues and associations.

Your professional colleagues are an often-overlooked source of information about your community and/or the problem(s) you are addressing. When attending professional meetings, reading professional bulletins and newsletters, or simply chatting with colleagues, always listen for innovative interpretations and techniques for identifying and quantifying needs in the community.

(9) Review the literature.

A thorough review of current literature addressing the same and/or similar problem(s) you are considering can be beneficial. By reading the methodologies, approaches, and solutions reported by other agencies, you can often identify additional needs and barriers that impact your community. Studying programs that worked and did not work in other locations can provide new perspectives for your community's problems.

Use the Internet as a research tool. Literature and information searches that used to require several days and trips to large libraries now take only a few hours. It is imperative that you (or someone on your grants development team) have the necessary patience and skill to successfully surf the Internet.

(10) Create a newspaper clippings file.

Do not underestimate the value of using recent articles in local, regional, or even national newspapers to identify and assess community needs. Oftentimes, newspapers investigate reports about local problems, and news headlines, articles, statistics, and quotes can provide documented evidence of local needs.

It is a good practice for every grantwriter to create and maintain a file of newspaper clippings, including any headline or article that portrays local needs. The more negative the story, the stronger the potential for assisting in both conducting community needs assessments and in writing the Problem Statement. Watch for articles that track negative economic or health trends, poor ratings of any kind, poor scholastic performance, and high crime statistics, to name a few.

For example, The State newspaper in Columbia, S.C., ran these headlines: "S.C. Has Little Success Saving Children's Lives," "Summer School Budgets to Take a Hit," and "S.C. Has Worst Death Rate from Accidents in Nation." In USA Today we saw "Portrait of a Town in Trouble." (Unfortunately, we have not yet engaged clients from that particular community, so we have not been able to use the headline as a citation—but it did make a compelling phrase when incorporated into one of our grants!)

Developing Convincing Problem Statements

Making Reviewers Cry!

Begin writing the Problem Statement by first informing the reader what problem your proposal is addressing, with a clear, concise statement of the problem. Next, briefly identify the cause(s) of the problem and your prediction of its long-term effects. Then, transition into a discussion of the problem supported by facts and statistics.

Opening the Problem Statement is easy if you use the three simple statements below:

The problem is ... *state the problem.*

The problem is caused by ... *state the cause of the problem.*

Long-term and without intervention ... *state long-term consequences if no intervention occurs.*

Let's consider an example. Suppose the problem your agency wants to address is that a rural elementary school serving predominantly low-income students has no afterschool programs. As a result, many young children are home alone in the afternoons, unsupervised by adults. These children are mostly from single-parent families and the parents are at work in the afternoons. It does not take much imagination to predict dire long-term consequences such as children failing to complete homework assignments, falling behind academically, misbehaving at school, experimenting with alcohol and other drugs, getting suspended, dropping out of school, turning to crime, and possibly going to prison. The Problem Statement could be written as follows:

> **The problem is** that many students who attend Smith Elementary School are home alone and lack adult supervision in the afternoons.

> **The problem is caused by** a lack of afterschool programs available for low-income students in the target area.

> **Long-term and without intervention**, many of these students will fall behind academically, develop behavior problems, get suspended, drop out of school, abuse drugs, and possibly end up in prison!

After you have set forth the problem, its causes, and its consequences if ignored, you need to be expand on each of these areas with details that support your analysis. The recommendations that follow will help you develop a convincing Problem Statement.

▶▶ *Personalize the community's needs.*

Your goal in writing the Problem Statement is to tell the story of your target community, describing community problems and issues in a compelling manner. You want to convince the reader that unmet needs are critical and action is clearly required.

We recommend you write as though you are a member of the community. Use the words "we" and "our" to personalize the problem and engage the reader in its solution. For example, do not write, "The senior citizens in Green County live by themselves;

many lack transportation." Write, "Our elderly live alone, many isolated by their lack of transportation."

▶▶ *Compel the reviewer to help your target population.*

High-scoring proposals make the reviewer want to assist in solving the problem. To encourage this sentiment, we frequently use strong, emotional language such as "misery index" and "poorest of the poor" to describe the intense needs of our target population.

One of our training participants reported she had participated as a federal reviewer in a recent grants competition. She was reading a proposal from Arkansas in which the need was so compelling she reported, "I wanted to leave the hotel, fly to Arkansas, and help those people!"

When questioned further, she told us she had rated the Arkansas proposal very highly and worthy of funding. This is exactly what we want to achieve.

▶▶ *Employ statistics to prove the need.*

Use the best—that is, the most persuasive—statistics uncovered during your needs assessment to document your problem strongly and clearly. We also recommend you employ statistics from several different, independent sources—four or five is best. Always cite the date and source for every statistic you employ. (We'll discuss methods for citations and references in Step10.)

▶▶ *Chart significant statistics for emphasis.*

Graphs and charts can be excellent tools for emphasizing your statistics. Be sure they are clear and easily understood. We strongly recommend, however, you limit graphics to no more than one per page to keep the text from appearing too choppy.

A recent Research Associates proposal included the following introductory paragraph and graphic:

According to the United Health Foundation's State Health Ranking (2004), South Carolina ranks 49th worst in the nation in high school graduation. In one of our targeted school districts, planners predict that of the 500 freshmen currently enrolled, more than 60% will not graduate! As shown in the chart below, the dropout rate in each of our five coalition schools far exceeds the state average of 25%.

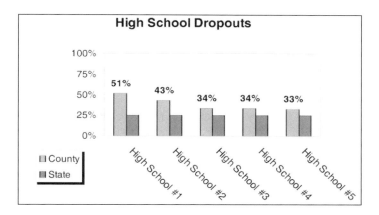

RA Tip! Keep in mind these tools will draw the eye of the reviewer, so use them to illustrate only your most significant findings.

►► *Use tables and lists.*

Long paragraphs containing many statistics–however compelling–will often lose the attention of the reviewer. (Remember that reviewers are prone to scanning as they review many grants in a short period of time.) Two techniques will lessen the impact of this problem and place more suitable emphasis on your most significant findings: tables and bulleted lists.

The following sample descriptions are drawn from a recent Problem Statement in a funded proposal developed by Research Associates. Sample One has been modified as a statistics discussion limited to text only. Sample Two (from the actual proposal) combines introductory text and a table. Sample Three illustrates the same information in a bulleted format.

Sample One: Text Only

Significant levels of poverty characterize South Carolina in every national comparison. Sadly, Target County ranks worst in the state for almost every poverty indicator. At 44%, Target County ranks worst for children under 18 living below poverty and nearly twice the state rate of 23%. Target also rates a distressing 73% (also worst in the state) for children below 200% of poverty and has 35% of its overall population living in poverty. Other economic measures reveal 52% of Target children living in single-parent families (more than twice the state rate), and retail sales at a dismal $4,653 per capita (about half of the $8,874 state rate). Household isolation is defined by the nearly 40% of families without a telephone (compared to 9% statewide), and 1 of every 4 families lacks an automobile (compared to 1 of 10 statewide).

Kids Count (2004) reports that "poverty often traps families in dependency. Many poor families have barriers such as lack of transportation or a phone that prevent them from being self sufficient." These factors are familiar problems to Target County families. Further, school district surveys report that 78% of students in Target County have no access to transportation (2004).

Sample Two: Text and Table

Significant levels of poverty characterize South Carolina in every national comparison. Sadly, Target County ranks worst in the state for almost every poverty indicator. For example, Target County ranks worst for children under 18 living below poverty. Target also rates a distressing 73% (also worst in the state) for children below 200% of poverty. The following table reflects the "misery index" of Target County.

Poverty Indicators *	S.C.	Target County
Children (0-17) Living below Poverty	23 %	44 %
Population below Poverty	15 %	35 %
Children in Single-Parent Families	25 %	52 %
Retail Sales per Capita	$8,874	$4,653
Households with No Telephone	9 %	19 %
Households with No Car	11 %	25 %

* Statistics from Kids Count 2004, U.S. Bureau of the Census (2000)

Kids Count (2004) reports that "poverty often traps families in dependency. Many poor families have barriers such as lack of transportation or a phone that prevent them from being self sufficient." These factors are familiar problems to Target families. In Target County, these statistical indicators are twice that of the state's average (see table above), and school district surveys report that 78% of students have no access to transportation (2004).

Sample Three: Text and Bulleted List

Significant levels of poverty characterize South Carolina in every national comparison. Sadly, Target County ranks worst in the state for almost every poverty indicator. For example, Target County ranks worst for children under 18 living below poverty. Target also rates a distressing 73% (also worst in the state) for children "below 200% of poverty." The following statistics reflect the "misery index" of Target County compared to the state:

- Children (0-17) living below poverty in S.C. (23%) and Target (44%)
- Population below poverty in S.C. (15%) and Target (35%)
- Children in single-parent families in S.C. (25%) and Target (52%)
- Retail sales per capita in S.C. ($8,874) and Target ($4,653)

- Households with no telephone in S.C. (9%) and Target (19%)
- Households with no car in S.C. (11%) and Target (25%)

Kids Count (2004) reports that "poverty often traps families in dependency. Many poor families have barriers such as lack of transportation or a phone that prevent them from being self sufficient." These factors are familiar problems to Target families. In Target County, these statistical indicators are twice that of the state's average (see above list), and school district surveys report that 78% of students have no access to transportation (2004).

If you were a tired reviewer, scanning these sample Problem Statements, which statistics would catch your attention most effectively? We believe Sample Two is best and Sample Three is second best. Do you see how the statistics in Sample One get lost in the text?

▶▶ *Make the numbers catch the reader's attention.*

How you present numerical data can also be a factor in the reader's comprehension of community problems. The techniques listed below will assist you in proving your needs.

- ▶ **Numerals:** In the Problem Section, write all numbers as figures to help them stand out and catch the attention of the readers. For example, write "The council predicts that 60% of the elderly population will be homebound" rather than "sixty percent."

- ▶ **Integers:** Use whole numbers and avoid decimal places most of the time. (Employ standard rounding, with less than .5 rounded down and .5 or greater rounded up to the next whole number.) The average reader will not note any difference between 13% and 13.3%.

- ▶ **Tangibles:** Examine the numbers you are citing and express them in the manner that will provide the most lasting impression for the reader. For example, if you know that 64% of families are affected by a problem, consider stating "nearly 2/3 of our families" or "2 out of every 3 families."

► **Perception:** Apply the same psychology sales people have used for years—the first decimal is the most important for perception (e.g., $50 is too much to spend, but $49.95 is affordable!). We refer to this as the "Blue Light Special" approach to statistics. Why report that hunger affects 48% of the children when you can report honestly—and with much more impact—that nearly half the children go to bed hungry?

►► *Close the Problem Statement with a ray of hope.*

Having written a Problem Statement that will make reviewers cry, you want to shift emotional gears for a more hopeful closing. Why? We believe most reviewers read—and then score—each proposal, section by section. Thus, while we do want reviewers to feel moved by the Problem Statement, we don't want them so depressed they score negatively, believing your targeted situation is hopeless. For this reason, we recommend you end this section with a closing paragraph (or at least a sentence or two) offering some hope. The wrap-up or closing statements may include a summary of your findings, offer closure to the problem, and suggest that solutions do exist. This sample paragraph provided closure to the Problem Statement in a recent, successful proposal by Research Associates:

> Our comprehensive needs assessment verifies there are large numbers of children and parents experiencing serious and growing levels of poverty, unemployment, illiteracy, health, and social problems. As the number and quality of available jobs has decreased, the incidence of poverty and illiteracy has increased. We are left with a vicious cycle that perpetuates itself in the form of hopelessness. To break this devastating cycle, children must be prepared to enter school, parents must find jobs, and local employers must find qualified employees. A skill gap divides them, but a comprehensive family literacy program will bridge that gap.

In Closing: Always remember that your proposed program activities are not mentioned in the Problem Statement. Your program is good news, and the Problem Statement is purposefully focused on bad news, leading the reader to yearn for the solution—your program. Step 4 explains how to develop program strategies and present them in the Approach.

After you have thoroughly described the problem(s) challenging the target population, your grant proposal will shift into a positive gear as you describe the program strategies your agency will use to address the problem(s) and help the community. This is the most important fundamental difference between grantwriting and fundraising. Grantwriters seek monies to fund programs that will *make the world a better place* by addressing community problems. Fundraisers focus their efforts on getting money to buy things or meet goals. Although their agencies may help others, their efforts to raise money are focused on the agency and its needs–not the program and the community's needs.

This section of the grant proposal is known by several names including **Program Strategies**, **Project Activities**, **Program Design**, **Project Narrative**, and the **Approach**. "Approach" —which we will use in this book— is a slightly older federal term that succinctly describes this portion of your proposal where your approach to reducing the problem is described.

RA Note: The term Project Narrative may be confusing to newer grantwriters because the entire written portion of a grant proposal is also commonly referred to as the Project Narrative. In this usage, the terms differentiating between the sections of the application written in paragraph style (the Project Narrative) versus the required forms and/or appendices of the application.

> ### Caution: Keep Your Focus Realistic!
>
> Keep in mind that the types of societal problems addressed by most grant programs will never be completely eliminated. Rather, they will be positively impacted by your efforts: decreased, reduced, improved, or prevented.
>
> We reviewed one proposal in which overly enthusiastic planners promised that for $10,000, they would reduce the crime rate by half in their community. While $10,000 could fund some very effective programs, including youth basketball leagues or crime watch programs, it is very unlikely crime rates will drop that sharply as a result of a $10,000 investment.

Searching for Ideas

What in the World Are You Going to Do?

In some ways, designing the Approach is similar to conducting the needs assessment. Several methods for creating an innovative and realistic Approach mirror the techniques suggested for assessing community needs. However, your focus is different as you review existing program ideas, seeking potential program components that will address your identified community needs.

▶▶ *Review the literature.*

In designing your program, a review of the current research in your field is a must for several reasons. First, it is a source of innovative ways to attract and engage the target population and to deliver services. Remember, creativity is often the key to extra points from reviewers and funders who are often neither excited by nor interested in funding the "same old" approaches to problems. Second, the use of current research will lend validity and credibility to your proposal, another way to earn those extra points.

The Internet offers immediate access to articles, abstracts, professional journals, books, conference minutes, and white papers on almost any topic imaginable. Depending upon your area of programming, you may also need to conduct more traditional library research to obtain professional and national-organization resources.

Sample Resource Websites

The Internet Public Library, located at **www.ipl.org**, is very user-friendly and maintains an extensive collection of online references.

ERIC, the Educational Resources Information Center, located at **www.eric.ed.gov**, is one of the major bibliographic databases worldwide with an abundance of articles and research documents available on a wide range of topics.

And don't forget that powerful search engines such as those at **www.google.com**, **www.dogpile.com**, **www.yahoo.com**, or **www.msn.com** are excellent places to begin your search.

In several fields, **Best Practices** and **Promising Practices** are collected and published by the professional authorities as innovative solutions to community problems. In general, Best Practices are those that have been successfully implemented in multiple settings with proven results. Promising Practices have usually demonstrated limited success, but have not yet achieved the validity with as many successful replications as those that qualify as Best Practices. Many reviewers will award bonus points to applications for programs that are implementing either Best or Promising Practices strategies since these offer higher probabilities for successful program implementation.

Use the Internet to find Best Practices in your area of interest. A recent Internet search for "Best Practices" yielded more than three million hits. Sample topics included Youth Violence Prevention, Classroom Management, Mentoring, Ambulatory and Clinical Care of HIV-Infected Patients, Nursing Excellence, Vocational Education, HUD-What Works in Communities, Clinical Excellence, National Association of Regional Councils, Local Leadership, Comprehensive Tobacco Control Programs, Special Needs Opportunity Windows, Learning Reading, Building

Successful Prevention Programs, Students with Disabilities, Human Resources, Respite Services, Public Safety, and many others.

▶▶ *Interview experts and professionals.*

Some say an expert is "someone who knows more about a topic than you do." This statement reminds us that there are many experienced providers in almost every community who have delivered successful programs serving some members of your target population. Although their focus and goals may have been different from yours, their input is valid nonetheless. Seek them out and solicit their advice. Find out what worked and what did not work in their program approaches and why. For example, if you are developing a proposal to improve infant delivery weights and address the problems associated with low-birth-weight babies, a neonatologist would be an excellent local expert for consultation.

Beyond your immediate community, there are experts and professionals both within your state and nationally who are familiar with programming activities addressing problems similar to yours. Also consider the advice of professionals from other fields, because their successful programs may translate into a successful, innovative approach for your program. For example, engaging the target population is problematic for many new programs. Your program planning can benefit from the solutions of other service providers as well as those employed by the faith and business communities.

Professional grants development firms may also be helpful in developing strategies and innovative approaches. With their broader base of experience and familiarity with research techniques, this type of firm is generally an asset to the planner of new programs. Many grants development firms offer consulting services (e.g., planning sessions and meeting facilitation) in addition to grantwriting services.

▶▶ *Attend relevant conferences.*

Keep your antenna tuned for conferences and seminars (local, regional, and national) that bring together professionals, lay persons, researchers, volunteers, funding source staff, and/or service recipients who are interested in solutions to the same challenges and issues you are addressing. Formal sessions often present the latest research. Further, informal conversations with other attendees can provide ideas about approaches you might use.

Conferences and meetings outside your program area can also be fertile fishing grounds. Many planners prefer to "troll" for ideas from unusual sources that can then be adapted to projects as needed.

▶▶ *Interview consumers and community key informants.*

One of the most often overlooked avenues for developing program ideas is the solicitation of input from the target population. Never assume that "if they knew how to solve the problems, they would have done so." Many of the most successful grant proposals facilitate community empowerment. In these instances, by providing necessary resources, the grant creates the opportunity for a community to solve its own problems.

Similar to methods for assessing community needs (previously discussed in Step 3), techniques such as surveys, focus groups, and interviews with community key informants set the stage for community empowerment and facilitate program implementation. Establishing a basis for community "buy-in" is an important and often critical step in planning a successful program.

It is a good practice for grantwriters to attend meetings of all types in their community—county council meetings, civic associations, church groups, and others. Many of these larger gatherings provide forums for community members to express their ideas freely, offering fantastic resources for planning grant programs.

▶▶ *Review funded grant proposals.*

There are several methods you can employ to obtain copies of funded grant proposals. Keep in mind that prior to public funding, the technology (or work product) of the grant application or proposal belongs to the applicant agency or individual. However, after government proposals or applications are funded or approved, they become public domain and may be obtained under the Freedom of Information (FOI) laws.

▶ **Federal Grants:** Many website for federal funding opportunities offer samples of funded applications that can be reviewed and even downloaded and printed for additional study. However, not all funded proposals provided online meet our high grantwriting standards. Thus, we suggest you exercise caution in using funded grants as models. Remember that these proposals often represent applications from the first year of funding, which may be slightly less competitive than subsequent years.

▶ **State/County/Local Grants:** Availability of funded proposals varies widely from one locale to another. Your best approach is to contact the grants or program officer (usually listed in the RFP) and inquire about the availability of funded or sample proposals. Be sure to ask about proposals that were funded in prior competitions and/or previous years.

▶ **Foundation/Corporation Grants:** These grant programs do not fall under public domain, and some foundations and corporations are reluctant to share funded proposals while others share freely. For example, a Research Associates vice president who is a former foundation director reports encouraging potential applicants to come in to review grants and even make copies of funded applications. When communicating with the foundation office, just ask if they provide samples of funded applications or allow potential grant applicants to come in and read funded proposals. You may get lucky!

Keep in mind also the Annual Report of most foundations or corporations will list the current grantees, and many will include contact information. It is well worth your time to scan these lists and consider contacting a few successful applicants for their programming advice. For example, a library in North Dakota might gladly share a funded grant with a library in Florida since they are not likely to compete for the same funding.

▶▶ *Contact and visit existing programs.*

Nothing beats seeing a program in action for triggering a flow of ideas about what will—and will not—work in your agency. A few years ago at Research Associates, we developed our first grant proposal for a school district seeking funds to establish an Even Start program. Even Start is a comprehensive concept that combines family literacy and child development by focusing on four tenets: parent literacy, early childhood literacy, parenting, and the Parent And Child Together (PACT) program. Despite our in-depth review of available Even Start literature, we did not fully comprehend or appreciate the concept of the Even Start model until we located and visited an existing center. The visit was truly an "Aha!" experience as we observed first hand how the program operated. This experience empowered us to recognize the potential of this unique style of delivering comprehensive family-literacy services, resulting in a successful grant proposal.

If a site visit is not possible, try to at least talk with program managers of projects that could provide ideas for your planning.

Developing the Program Model
Getting Your Act Together

After completing your research, it's time to identify program components, or activities, and organize them into the program model. This model will serve as the foundation for the Approach narrative.

It is essential that model components be presented logically and clearly. Among the thousands of grants we have reviewed, some of the worst proposals are those that, although enthusiastic and creative, lack organization in their presentation.

One straightforward way to organize your program components is as simple as arranging them into a chronological outline. The following steps will assist you in this process:

➤ **List:** Begin by creating a list naming every possible component of your program. Try to imagine every step involved. For example, if clients (or patients, participants, consumers, etc.) must come to you, will they require transportation services? How will this transportation be provided?

➤ **Order:** Now, arrange your list items chronologically (in the order in which each program component will occur during your project).

➤ **Expand:** Next, apply the "Six Ws of Writing" (who, what, why, when, where, and how) to each component. For example, consider a program that will include outreach services for clients. Ask, Who will identify and engage clients? What types of services will be provided? Why do we need outreach services? When (or on what schedule) will we offer the services? Where will we provide these services (consumer homes, community centers, or satellite clinics)? How will we transport our staff? Each answer will provide valuable planning information and some may elicit additional components.

➤ **Review:** As a last step, review your program several times from different perspectives, making sure every necessary activity has been addressed. Consider the viewpoints of your agency administrators, project manager, service providers, potential clients, engaged clients, and referring agencies in the community. Ask yourself if your model is complete.

For example, if you were planning a program to provide health screening for senior citizens in your community, what components would you include? You might list transportation, health screenings, advisory committee, volunteers, and the target population.

Now, arrange these components in chronological order: (1) form an advisory committee; (2) identify the target population; (3) solicit community volunteers to identify and engage clients; (4) develop arrangements for transporting clients to and from agency; and (5) perform health screenings.

As you continue to review and improve your model, you might realize step three is actually two steps: (a) the recruitment of volunteers, and (b) the identification and engagement of clients. Later you might decide identification and engagement of clients are two separate components. A health practitioner would point out that you need to decide what to do with the results of the screenings, so you add a component addressing referrals for additional services.

In this manner, your program model continues to evolve until all program planners agree all components have been identified and included.

RA Secret! The program model you develop will serve as an excellent resource not only for writing your Approach section but also as a valuable reference when defining personnel needs and drafting the program budget.

Writing a Successful Approach

Bringing Your Program to Life

Unlike the Problem Statement with its gloom and doom outlook, the Approach takes on a positive and exciting note. Your enthusiasm and creativity in bringing your program to life should be reflected in an upbeat, well-planned presentation of program ideas, and your writing should compel the reader to keep reading.

Your goal in writing the Approach is to tell the reader what you are going to do about the problem(s) you have described. You should describe how your program will be implemented and how it will impact community problems. Your narrative should be based on your logically developed program model and should fully describe each component of the proposed project. Remember that writing the Approach is similar to giving a speech, and the familiar public-speaking adage applies:

1. Tell the audience what you are going to say.
2. Say it.
3. Summarize what you just said!

Seven Secrets for a Successful Approach

The One with the Most Points Wins!

(1) Begin with the goals of the grant program.

We recommend that you begin the Approach by stating the goals, or purpose, of the grant program. Basically, the goals identify what you plan to accomplish with your project. Many successful writers make their program goals mirror the goals stated in the RFP. Keep in mind that when stating the RFP goals, funders are essentially revealing what they want to buy, or fund, with their grant dollars. It stands to reason, therefore, that by incorporating the goals of the funding source in your proposal, you will improve your chances of meeting their funding criteria and getting funded.

For example, your state department of health and human services might fund a program "for the purpose of decreasing infant mortality." As an administrator in your county health department, you know your county has low birth weights and high percentages of teen (and pre-teen) pregnancies. Thus, you may design a program with components targeting adolescent prevention and prenatal care with a program goal of "decreasing infant mortality."

Most RFPs refer to the overall purpose or mission of your grant project as the goal(s) of your program, and some will use terms such as vision or mission for the overall goal. We prefer the more commonly used term, goal. (The final development of your program goal(s) and their associated objects will be fully addressed in Step 5.)

(2) Provide a program overview.

Early in the Approach, you should introduce the reader to your project and its activities with an overview of the program. This provides readers with the "big picture" perspective as they begin to read the details of various program components.

Little is more frustrating in reviewing a grant proposal than a program description that jumps from one component to another with no apparent relationship between them. The writer whose Approach begins by describing activities such as recruiting businessmen as volunteers, providing field trips, establishing regular recreational activities, and soliciting input from community leaders will confuse a reviewer who has not been told how the program activities relate to the purpose or goals of the program.

(3) Include an advisory committee.

It is always a good idea to include an advisory or planning committee both in developing your proposal and in writing your Approach. Not only will this element enhance your planning efforts, but it will also gain favor with reviewers, earning points during the scoring process. Advisory committees are best composed of a cross section of community key informants, agency personnel, service providers, and potential consumers of services. They provide agency and community accountability for the proposed program as well as oversight and guidance for program planning, implementation, and management. This group is sometimes referred to as a "task force," which the advisory committee may appoint for program oversight once funding has been granted. If you have an existing planning group in place, use this group in your grant proposal. Chances are, they already understand your organization and its mission, saving you the time required to educate a new committee.

When developing an advisory committee, be sure to review the RFP again. Occasionally, an RFP will not only encourage an advisory committee for program planning and/or implementation, but it will also suggest specific desirable attributes (for example, the socio-economic make up of this committee).

In the Approach, the advisory committee should be described "generically." This means describing each member according to their relevant professional or personal attributes rather than by name. For example, rather than listing Mr. John Smith of XYZ Industries, describe this member as the human resources manager for XYZ Industries. Rather than Rev. John Brown, state that the member is the pastor of a large local church.

RA Secret! The advisory committee is often the first program component described in the Approach. This is because the Approach is developed in chronological order, and program planning is usually provided by or overseen by the advisory committee. Be sure to describe both the role and the relevance of the advisory committee in your proposal so reviewers will appreciate the accountability it will provide for your project.

(4) Describe the target population.

A critical component of the Approach is the description of the target population, the group the program is going to serve. This description should begin with the broader, more general definition such as applicable geographic boundaries. For example, a project may plan to serve senior citizens enrolled in a specific eldercare program, senior citizens living in a clearly delineated neighborhood or housing project, or all senior citizens in the county.

After you have identified the broad parameters defining the target population, you must describe the selection criteria that will be employed for inclusion of persons into the grant program. The purpose for each selection criterion should also be explained. For example, your program may target families in HUD-subsidized housing in a specific geographic location. Within that group, you may be interested in serving only families having both pre-school children and a stay-at-home parent.

Some programs serve **primary** and **secondary** populations. Consider an adolescent drug court treatment program in which parents or guardians must participate in weekly court appearances and the entire family receives counseling services. In this case, the juvenile offenders are the primary target population and both the parents or guardians and the siblings are secondary populations. We recommend that you review your program model carefully to identify any secondary populations. Recognizing that your program will serve a secondary population will increase the size of the impacted population, which may be a selling point for the proposal.

RA Secret! An often-overlooked aspect of describing the target population is your description of how your agency is going to identify potential consumers as well as engage them into program services. Too often, the novice grantwriter simply assumes that if a program is created, participants will appear. Unfortunately, this oversight is the downfall of many programs, as we have learned.

For example, in one Research Associates funded proposal, a school district with a high percentage of African Americans reached program capacity within a matter of weeks of their initial recruiting efforts. Another district using the same grant model served a high percentage of Hispanic families. Several months into the program, this school district had only recruited three families (and none of these were attending regularly). It turned out that in this Hispanic community, women were not encouraged to obtain a good education. Thus, families were not receptive to a family literacy program that offered educational opportunities for the mothers of high-risk children. In this case, program implementation suffered because we failed to recognize the enormous impact of cultural differences.

(5) *Cite the literature.*

We have discussed the importance of a literature review in exploring program models and developing your project strategy. In writing the Approach, we recommend that you cite at least five sources relevant to the strategies you have planned. If applicable, it can also be beneficial to reference national models (such as Best or Promising Practices, discussed earlier in this chapter). Although citations of current literature have always been important, it has recently become even more so. The current trend among grantors, both private and governmental, is towards preferring—and often requiring—proposals to employ scientifically based research methodologies in their planned strategies. Your ability to demonstrate familiarity with current research and your integration of this knowledge into your project planning add both validity and credibility to your program and its planners. This is a sure way to gain points during review.

As you review the literature, remember to keep a detailed account of where and how you obtained the references. Whether or not your proposal includes a formal bibliography, you should always be able to identify and locate every source you cite. (In Step 11, we recommend methods for citations within the text and also in a reference page.)

This aspect of the Approach should not seem daunting. Reference citation is similar to writing the high school, college, or graduate research papers familiar to most of us. The sample below is excerpted from a recently funded Research Associates proposal.

> Our primary emphasis is a basic restructuring of our large high school to create smaller learning communities within the existing school in response to the large body of research agreeing that "smaller is better." The literature indicates that "students in small schools earn better grades, fail fewer courses, miss fewer days, and are much less likely to drop out of school than students in large schools" (Wolk, 2001). The ability of smaller groups to know each other and care about

the students appears critical. Cotton (2000) reports, "People in small schools come to know and care about one another to a greater degree than is possible in large schools, and rates of parent involvement are higher."

Creating smaller learning environments is particularly appropriate for the high-poverty populations served by our coalition. Howley (2000) reported that "smaller schools reduce the damaging effects of poverty on student achievement and help students from poorer communities narrow the achievement gap between them and students from wealthier communities." The Rural School and Community Trust (2000) concluded "schools with smaller enrollments consistently and significantly outperformed larger ones when it came to the achievement of children from low-income families."

(6) Ensure activities relate to problems.

As you develop your program model, delineating the strategies and activities you plan to implement, always keep in mind the problems identified in your Problem Statement and their relationship to your program. Using the jargon of consultants, grant projects tend to be vulnerable to "scope creep" as enthused planners add more and more helpful components to serve the target population. This project expansion is not a bad thing as programs targeting community problems must often deal with numerous interrelated problems requiring a variety of program strategies. However, it is important that the activities that you present in your proposed Approach clearly relate to the problems identified in the Problem Statement.

If, for example, you are working with adolescents in a violence-reduction program and plan to include a mentoring component, your Problem Statement may indicate the percentage of area students from single-parent homes, and your selection criteria (for inclusion into the program) might include points for students from single-parent families. You may also identify the absence or low number of role models among the targeted students as a precipitating factor in some of the problems being experienced.

Thus, the lack of available role models provides sound justification for providing program youth with mentors.

(7) Justify the chosen strategies.

In writing the Approach, tell the reader why you are doing each activity, even though it may seem obvious. You want to clarify the relationship between the program components and the problems identified earlier in the proposal. You should not assume the reader will interpret the problems or the research in the same manner you have. Further, you should never assume the reader implicitly understands the relationships between appalling demographics and underlying causes. For this reason, the Approach should clearly explain these relationships, leading the reader to understand (and hopefully concur with) your conclusions, that is, your choice of program strategies.

For example, there is an established relationship between the descriptive demographic, "infant mortality rate," and the overall health, education, and socio-economic status of a community. However, readers may not be aware of this association and may not understand why you are citing this statistic in a program aimed at family literacy.

In the well-written proposal, there are no surprises for the reader. Relevant concepts are introduced appropriately throughout the proposal, and the solution proposed by the writer—the design of the project—makes sense to reviewers because they have been guided to draw the same conclusion.

In Closing: In our Logical Grantwriting Model, we have justified the need for the project and developed the program strategies we plan to implement. In Step 5, we will explore how to define the program goals and related objectives in a manner that wins the approval of reviewers. As we define the program goals, we will take into consideration the goals outlined in the RFP, the mission of our organization, our analysis of community needs, and the program that we are proposing.

STEP 5
DEFINING YOUR MISSION AND TASKS

As we discussed in Step 4, you should develop a statement for the Approach that summarizes the **mission** or **goal(s)** of your proposed program. This statement should reflect the interests of the funding source as expressed in the RFP program goals, and will establish the purpose of the program and context for the reviewer.

Earlier we said that goals expressed in the RFP reveal what funders want to buy or fund. Thus, your motive for basing your program and its goals on RFP goals is to improve your chances of being funded. We also noted that the RFP may speak in terms of a mission or vision rather than a goal, and your proposal would do well to reflect this language also. We will, however, continue to use the term "goal" for our purposes.

For each goal, you will need to develop **objectives** that state how you plan to reach the goal. These objectives consist of various activities or tasks that can be used to determine or measure success in attaining the goal.

Occasionally, we receive queries from our workshop participants who are surprised that program goals and objectives are not integrated into our grantwriting model until Step 5. These participants question, How can you identify the problem and describe your strategies if you do not know your program goals? Remember, this model is based on developing your proposal in the most logical manner and in the shortest amount of time. Although you should have a strong sense of your goals throughout program planning, you cannot explicitly or accurately express these thoughts until you have thought through your program strategies and written the Approach.

Writing Program Goals

How Will You Make the World a Better Place?

Program goals clarify your mission or what you plan to accomplish with your project and lay the foundation for justifying your program. Goals explain why your program is necessary by identifying *how your program will impact the target population.* In fact, goals tell how your project will make the world a better place. Despite the naïve optimism evoked by this last statement, keep in mind that grant programs are about improving conditions for the target population. *Grantwriting is not a profession for cynics.*

►► *How many goals are appropriate?*

Grantwriters are often uncertain as to how many goals should be addressed in a proposal. Research Associates recommends that one to four goals should suffice for almost any program. Keep in mind that typically, each goal has several objectives related to it. In general, larger programs (with a budget of more than $100,000) tend to have more goals, and smaller programs have fewer. However, we have seen many successful and comprehensive programs based on one simply expressed goal. On the other hand, too many goals may result in a proposal that lacks focus and confuses funders. In general, fewer is better.

►► *How specific should goals be?*

Another issue is gauging exactly how specific the language of the goal(s) should be. We recommend you begin a goals statement by specifying only the problem that you plan to address and the direction of the planned change. For example, your goal may be "to reduce highway deaths." In this case, the problem is highway mortality and the planned change is a reduction. This simple statement may suffice for your program. Remember, the elaboration and specifics will be addressed in the objectives.

Although goals can be expressed this succinctly, some elaboration may be helpful. The problem may require or benefit from additional definition, particularly in indicating the scope of your program. For example, the above goal changes in scope if expressed as "to reduce highway deaths in Texas" or "to reduce highway deaths in Texas attributed to DWI (driving while intoxicated)."

A common error among beginning grantwriters is introducing measurement into goal statements. Avoid this problem by keeping in mind that goals are visionary and are, therefore, not measurable. For this reason, *goal statements should not include numbers, percentages, deadlines, quotas, or dates for comparison. These will be identified in your program objectives.*

Sample Program Goals
- To increase awareness of cancer risk factors
- To reduce recidivism rates among adolescents
- To decrease hunger
- To improve local support for cultural events
- To decrease birth defects
- To prevent alcohol and other drug abuse

▶▶ *Where should goals statements be placed?*

We recommend program goals be stated in at least three locations in your grant proposal: (1) in any Abstract or Summary section of the project; (2) per Step 4, in the beginning of the Approach; and (3) again just prior to or as part of the introduction of program objectives (see "Create measurable objectives" in the next section.)

Also remember that the Research Associates Logical Grantwriting Model is the best method for developing and writing about your program components. Prior to submitting your proposal, each component of the proposal should then be rearranged according to the outline provided or implied by the RFP. The funding agency may provide guidelines as formal as an outline complete with numbering system, or as simple as an informal series of questions or issues to be addressed. Always strive to not only provide all information requested but to arrange it in the order that the reviewers will anticipate receiving it. The order specified or suggested by the RFP is mandatory for funding by most funders.

What we are saying is that you should "spoonfeed" or guide reviewers through the description of your program so they will not fail to see requested or required items that you have provided in the application. Unfortunately, it is not uncommon to receive calls from funding agencies after the proposal review process asking for information that is in the proposal! How to respond when this happens while maintaining your cool will be addressed in Step 12.

Our point here is that in addition to the three recommended locations, your program goals should be included in every proposal section in which the RFP mentions program goals.

RA Secret! It can also be helpful to indicate your focus on a program goal by incorporating it frequently throughout the proposal. For example, in the Approach, occasionally insert a "reminder" phrase such as "for the purpose of reducing highway deaths" into your description of program strategies.

▶▶ *Do larger programs require more complex goals?*

The goal statement alone does not indicate the size—or potential impact—of the program. It is the delineation of the objectives that begins to indicate the breadth of the program and the depth of the required funding.

For example, the program goal "to prevent substance abuse" may introduce a $10,000 program to conduct prevention activities among ten-year-olds in the community, or it may introduce a $10 million program with multiple strategies for all age groups community-wide.

However, larger and more comprehensive programs often have not only several goals but also goals that are described in more detail.

The goals below are excerpted from a successful proposal by Research Associates for a five-school-district coalition to implement a three-year, comprehensive Smaller Learning Communities program with multimillion dollar funding. Notice that despite its size, this program was based on only three goals.

With an identified mission of "raising the bar" for every high school student in order to engage students and improve academic achievement, graduation rates, career development, and post-secondary outcomes, the Planning Task Force, with membership from the five school districts, established three goals for our innovative and research-based SC CARES program:

Goal 1. School Climate: To create smaller, more personalized, and safer high school learning communities where teachers, staff, students, parents, and community organizations care about each other and work collaboratively to challenge students and to support learning.

Goal 2. Student Achievement: To assist all high school students in maximizing their academic potential as demonstrated by meeting the challenging South Carolina State Academic Standards.

Goal 3. Academic Rigor, Student Retention, and Career Development: To help ensure that all students not only graduate but do so equipped with the necessary knowledge and skills for a successful transition into a post-secondary education, training, and/or careers.

Developing Program Objectives
How Will You Get There from Here?

Well-written objectives specify the minimum measures of what must be accomplished in order to meet your goals. What this means is that the objectives actually provide your definition of program success.

►► *Clearly associate objectives with goals.*

Each project objective should be linked to a specific goal. If your program has multiple goals, we recommend you use a numbering system that reflects this relationship. For example, if you have three goals and there are two objectives associated with the first goal, they might be labeled Objective 1A and Objective 1B. This is a simple maneuver, but each step that clarifies your plan for reviewers is well worth the effort.

In general, project objectives should be presented the order in which they occur in the grant proposal. For example, in a prevention program, an objective to increase student awareness of the dangers of drugs as measured by pre/post testing would come after an objective to provide lessons and activities teaching these dangers.

RA Note: Grantwriters disagree as to how objectives should be numbered. Some prefer to list the objectives associated with each goal, perhaps using a combination of numeric and alphabetic characters as we have suggested above. Others prefer to present all objectives in chronological order and number them accordingly. Keep in mind that grantwriting is not an exact science; our foremost recommendation is that you present your objectives in the clearest manner possible so the reviewer readily understands your program goals and objectives.

►► *Create measurable objectives.*

To define the measures for success, every objective must specify a minimum trio of parameters, addressing who, what, and when for the expressed program component.

► **Who?** Identify the target population that will be affected. This includes those served in the program or qualified to receive program services.

► **What?** Clarify the planned activity or vehicle for change. For example, will the program provide direct, one-on-one services to selected individuals? If so, what type? Or will it be a media campaign aimed at an entire community?

➤ **When?** State the date by which this change will be accomplished and, when applicable, the time period for comparison.

Many objectives must also define two additional parameters: how many and how much.

➤ **How Many?** Specify how many individuals will be affected by the proposed activity. What is the number of participants you plan to impact or the number of services you plan to provide?

➤ **How Much?** Indicate how much change will occur. What is the percentage of change you plan to accomplish? What is the direction of this change: an increase or decrease? For example, you may plan to decrease the number of mothers presenting for hospital delivery without prenatal care by 10% when comparing last year's statistic to the occurrence the first year of your proposed outreach program.

➤➤ *Qualify the objective measures.*

Objectives must also explicitly define the minimum measures of success. This means they must specify the point beyond which success is attained. For this reason, your specific measures should be qualified by phrases such as "a minimum of" or "at least." This avoids the implication that the objective is met only if the exact number specified is accomplished.

> ### Using Qualifiers to Avoid a Pitfall
>
> Suppose an objective is worded "to provide transportation services for 100 elderly citizens in the county between 10/01/05 and 9/30/06." Would the objective be met if the program transported only 90 seniors? The answer is no. What if the program transported 120 seniors? Well, you might argue, the objective has not been met because "100 elderly citizens" implies exactly 100, not less and not more.
>
> A qualifier avoids this confusion. The objective would be better worded: "to provide transportation services for at least 100 elderly citizens in the county between 10/01/05 and 9/30/06."

▶▶ *Plan conservatively (under-promise and over-deliver).*

We consistently recommend that grantwriters under-promise and over-deliver. What we mean is that in planning/writing your objectives, you should use caution in projecting the scope or scale of your planned program's impact. In general, it is better to lower your estimated projections by 10 to 20 percent. This approach allows more flexibility during implementation, and you do not become derailed by minor delays; your conservative estimates have allowed for these unexpected glitches.

For example, if you think that during the first year of your Soup Kitchen you will provide 50 meals for the homeless, 2 days per week for 48 weeks (allowing 4 weeks for program startup), then you would calculate 50 x 2 x 48 = 4,800 meals. However, because many things happen to disrupt any program (severe weather, unexpected staff or volunteer absences, unanticipated problems engaging the target population, etc.), you might set your objective at 85 percent of 4,800, or 4,080 meals served during Year One. Your objective would be worded "To provide at least 4,080 meals for our city's homeless population from 07/01/05 to 06/30/06." (The "mechanics" of how many meals per day, days per week, etc., would have been expressed in program activities listed in the Approach.)

This same conservatism should be applied to rates of change. Many grantwriters estimate that increases or decreases of 10 to 20 percent in observed rates are reasonable estimates for effective programs that run one to three years. Further, in the field of prevention, experts now recommend that programs should not anticipate behavior change rates greater than 5 percent per year, particularly in the first year of a program.

For example, a program targeting smoking among middle school students may credibly predict a reduction of only 5 percent in the overall number of students who are smoking. The objective could be worded: "To reduce the number of students who have smoked in the last thirty days by 5% as measured by the biannual student assessment survey when comparing May 2005 and May 2006."

By the end of the program, if you had not had any disrupting glitches, then you may have actually delivered more than the conservatively estimated number of services or changed a rate by more than the predicted percent. In this happy circumstance, your program evaluation and your year-end reports and/or thank-you letter to your funding source can report glowingly that you achieved greater impact than you originally estimated. Your use of a conservative approach then results in your gaining credibility with the funder—critically important for future proposals. Always under-promise and over-deliver; you will not regret it.

RA Note: The conservative approach will often be a lifesaver during program evaluation. In Step 6, we will examine the close relationship between the program objectives and the evaluation plan.

▶▶ *Word objectives accurately.*

Writing objectives requires a delicate balancing act. On one hand, you must address all the relevant parameters specified above and include any requisite qualifiers to provide minimum measures of success for your program. On the other hand, you should avoid excessive language and unnecessary elaboration. Thus, your goal in constructing objectives is to word them as concisely as possible while ensuring they address all required parameters.

Remember that the numbers expressed in the objectives are the most important in your grant proposal because they tell the reviewer what impact your program will have on the target population. For this reason, you want these numbers to stand out and catch the attention of the reviewer. Thus, as in the Problem Statement, we recommend that you write all numbers as numerals; for example, "5" rather than "five." Similarly, use the percent sign, "%," rather than the word "percent." Thus, an objective could target a 5% increase or 10% reduction.

►► *Avoid the "B" word.*

Program objectives should be program-focused, not **budget**-oriented. An important tenet mentioned earlier in the Introduction bears repeating at this point. The basic difference between fundraising and grantwriting is fundraising may focus on the acquisition of assets, but grantwriters are seeking funding for a program to reduce or prevent a community problem. Keep this critical distinction foremost in your mind when expressing your objectives. Never mention buying something in a project objective (unless you are applying for an equipment grant).

►► *Understand process and outcome objectives.*

Now consider that these nonpurchasing, carefully worded, conservative, chronologically ordered, appropriately qualified, and parametrically measurable program objectives we have developed (whew!) may be classified as one of two basic types: **process objectives** or **outcome objectives**. There are several approaches used by professionals to define this dichotomy.

Some grantwriters describe process objectives as quantitative and outcome objectives as qualitative. Others explain that process objectives are generally short-term and outcome objectives are long-term. Let's take a closer look:

► **Process Objectives:** In general, process objectives measure quantitative accomplishments (i.e., things that are counted) and are often short-term in scope. Smaller projects tend to rely more on process objectives than their larger counterparts. Consider a program with the goal, "To improve the health of our senior citizens." A sample process objective is: "Objective 1A. To provide at least 240 health screenings for county residents, age 60 and older, during Year 1 of our program."

➤ **Outcome Objectives:** In contrast, outcome objectives reflect qualitative changes and are often more long-term in scope. These objectives may be harder to measure than process objectives as they often address changes in incidence rates or changes in behavior, attitude, or actions of the target population. In Step 6 we'll examine how evaluators deal with this challenge.

For the same goal, improving the health of seniors, a sample outcome objective is: "Objective 1B. To decrease the cholesterol levels of senior citizens by 5% when comparing screening levels from October 2005 and October 2006."

Let's consider another example (familiar to many of us) to illustrate the two types of objectives. Suppose you are planning to lose weight. The steps you would plan might include exercising four to five days per week and reducing caloric intake for some established period of time. These activities would be your process objectives. Your outcome objective: losing ten pounds.

One of our instructors prefers to express the difference between outcome and process objectives using a well-known saying: "To give a family fish is to feed them for a day; to teach a family to fish is to feed them for a lifetime."

A program serving a hungry village would have as one objective, to feed the people during the program (give them fish for each day). This is a short-term objective; when the program ends, so does the supply of fish. Also, the number of fish given can be counted, so this is a quantifiable process objective.

The same program would surely have as another objective, to teach the villagers how to fish, so they can eat beyond the time frame of the program. This is a long-term objective. You cannot "count" what happens, but a change occurs that impacts the quality of life in the village. This is a qualitative objective. And in the grant world, we would measure the percentage of villagers able to fish, pre- and post-program, to measure this change. This objective is an outcome objective.

Presenting the Objectives

Spoonfeed Those Reviewers!

One last point to consider in developing and writing objectives is how to present them. You want to make sure you capture and focus the reader's attention on them. Remember, your objectives are the heart of your proposal; they specify what you plan to do. Your other concern is clarity, making sure the reader understands what you are saying. There are several ways to present objectives, and your choice will depend on their number, complexity, and length.

Earlier in our discussion of goals, we showed a sample of three goals excerpted from a proposal for a five-district coalition to implement a three-year Smaller Learning Communities program. Here we show three ways of presenting the first goal of this program and the four objectives related to it. (As you review the three sample methods of presentation below, keep in mind that the actual proposal would also include Goal 2 with Objectives 2A, 2B, and 2C and Goal 3 with Objectives 3A, 3B, and 3C.)

Sample One: Paragraph Style

The Smaller Learning Community Coalition goals have been carefully interpreted in terms of objectives with specific and measurable student outcomes. These objectives are presented below with their corresponding goals.

GOAL 1, School Climate: to create smaller, more personalized, and safer high-school learning communities where teachers, staff, students, parents, and community organizations care about each other and work collaboratively to challenge students and to support learning. Objectives: (1A) to decrease the number of incidents of student violence in each of the five coalition high schools by at least 5% per school year for each year of the grant program; (1B) to decrease the number of incidents of alcohol and other drug use in each of the five coalition high schools by at least 5% per year for each year of the grant program; (1C) to decrease the number of expulsions, suspensions, and disciplinary actions in each of the five coalition high schools by at least 5% per school year of the grant program; and (1D) to increase the number of students involved in extracurricular activities in each of the five coalition high schools by at least 5% per school year for each year of the grant program.

Sample Two: Using a Bulleted List

The Smaller Learning Community Coalition goals have been carefully interpreted in terms of objectives with specific and measurable student outcomes. These objectives are presented below with their corresponding goals.

GOAL 1: School Climate. To create smaller, more personalized, and safer high-school learning communities where teachers, staff, students, parents, and community organizations care about each other and work collaboratively to challenge students and to support learning.

- **Objective 1A.** To decrease the number of incidents of student violence in each of the five coalition high schools by at least 5% per school year for each year of the grant program.

- **Objective 1B.** To decrease the number of incidents of alcohol and other drug use in each of the five coalition high schools by at least 5% per year for each year of the grant program.

- **Objective 1C.** To decrease the number of expulsions, suspensions, and disciplinary actions in each of the five coalition high schools by at least 5% per school year of the grant program.

- **Objective 1D.** To increase the number of students involved in extracurricular activities in each of the five coalition high schools by at least 5% per school year for each year of the grant program.

Sample Three: Table Presentation

The Smaller Learning Community Coalition goals have been carefully interpreted in terms of objectives with specific and measurable student outcomes. These objectives are expressed in the following table:

GOAL 1: School Climate. To create smaller, more personalized, and safer high-school learning communities where teachers, staff, students, parents, and community organizations care about each other and work collaboratively to challenge students and to support learning.	
Objective 1A	To decrease the number of incidents of student violence in each of the five coalition high schools by at least 5% per school year for each year of the grant program.
Objective 1B	To decrease the number of incidents of alcohol and other drug use in each of the five coalition high schools by at least 5% per year for each year of the grant program.
Objective 1C	To decrease the number of expulsions, suspensions, and disciplinary actions in each of the five coalition high schools by at least 5% per school year of the grant program.
Objective 1D	To increase the number of students involved in extracurricular activities in each of the five coalition high schools by at least 5% per school year for each year of the grant program.

RA Note: Model objectives typically include specific dates. The above example was from a multiyear proposal in which use of program years was an attempt to simplify objectives.

In most cases, a simple paragraph style like Sample One denies your objectives the focus they deserve. Objectives are important to your proposal; do not allow them to get lost in the text. If your program goal(s) and objectives are brief, you may consider paragraph formatting enhanced by some combination of boldface, underlining, and italics for emphasis. As you can see in Samples Two and Three, the bulleted list and the table are excellent means of directing the reader's focus to your objectives. Often, this choice depends upon the actual length of the objectives and the preference of the writer.

RA Secret! An advantage that you cannot see in these samples is the spacing advantage tables provide due to single-spaced text format. Many RFPs require the project narrative to be formatted with line spacing of 1.5 or higher. Single spacing in tables, however, is considered standard practice and an approved exception to line-spacing requirements. Further, tables often employ a font size that is one point smaller than the accompanying text. Both of these formatting exceptions allow you to present a lengthy set of goals and objectives in much less space when using the table format (we will discuss this in greater detail in Step 11).

Most grantwriters will quickly learn that a proposal written to address all of the recommendations given in our model will almost always tend to be longer than the maximum number of pages allowed in the RFP for the project narrative. Thus, space constraints are the enemy of the grantwriter, and techniques for reducing space are our allies.

In Closing: The careful crafting of your goals and objectives is critical to laying the foundation for program evaluation. In Step 6 we will address how your proposal will establish the components for evaluation of your program.

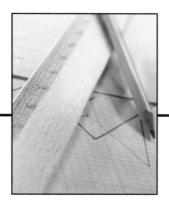

STEP 6
DESIGNING
THE EVALUATION

Novice grantwriters sometimes question why program evaluation must be included in the grant proposal or application. Their thinking is something like this: Evaluation will not happen until after we've finished our program. We'll simply decide how well we did and tell the funding source. Well, as they sing in the musical, My Fair Lady, "Wouldn't It Be Loverly?"

At Research Associates, we believe the evaluation component is critical to quality program design and successful grantwriting. It is in designing your evaluation that you establish both the mechanism and the tools not only for evaluation but also for program oversight and management. We strongly recommend that every grant proposal include an evaluation component—even if the RFP does not require one. By doing so, you will gain the approval of reviewers as you reveal your management expertise. This approval should translate into extra points when your proposal is scored. *Those extra points add up to a winning grant!*

►► *The dual purposes of program evaluation.*

To many grantwriters, the sole purpose of program evaluation is to answer the question, Did we accomplish what we planned based on the measurable objectives in our proposal? The evaluation provides the grantee and the funding source with measures for the level of program success.

We agree with this interpretation, but only as the prevailing purpose of evaluation, **not** the sole purpose. We believe quality program managers also employ evaluation to serve a second function, important because it impacts the project's overall success or failure: using evaluation to provide information to management. This means allowing evaluators to provide ongoing feedback to management at regular intervals throughout the life of the program. Evaluators regularly assess the progress of the program and provide information to grantees about how the project is performing and when it is deviating from the management plan. In addition, evaluators suggest when and how to implement changes to guide the project towards its established goal.

In discussing program evaluation, we must also consider the concept of accountability. It has been at least three decades since government grants began to include accountability as a factor in funding decisions. This trend met with resistance in some arenas. For example, federally subsidized healthcare programs were required to report the number of patient "encounters" for face-to-face patient-provider contacts. However, some physicians reacted negatively, believing that reporting patient "encounters" rather than "visits" was dehumanizing healthcare delivery. On the other hand, astute program managers embraced the move towards accountability, relieved that quality programs providing more services per dollar spent might be rewarded for their fiscal efficiency as well as for program success. Today's program planners address accountability concerns with the inclusion of an evaluation component.

►► *Communication between planners and evaluators.*

There should be close communication between the evaluation team and planners throughout the development of the project proposal. At Research Associates, we believe the evaluators should be identified early in the grantwriting process and actively involved in planning the grant. The role of evaluators during planning ensures the program goals are achievable because objectives are measurable and appropriately worded. Evaluator input is also helpful in developing the management plan (to be addressed in Step 8), especially since evaluators play an important role in the ongoing oversight and management of the program.

RA Note: In the grantwriting field, there is some debate about whether or not evaluators should be involved in the actual planning of a project. Some believe this is a conflict of interest, while others believe it makes good sense to involve the evaluators throughout the planning period. We believe the latter as it allows the evaluators to develop a sense of ownership in the program. This tends to promote the development of a strong evaluation model without comprising the integrity of the evaluation.

RA Tip! Occasionally, a rushed proposal may be funded that has not benefited from evaluator input. When this occurs, one of the first steps of competent program managers should be the careful review of the proposal by evaluators. This would be followed, if necessary, by the amendment of the original grant proposal or management plan.

►► *Engaging an independent evaluator.*

It is beyond the scope of this book to guide readers into qualifying as evaluators for grant programs. For this reason, our best advice is to engage the assistance of an independent evaluator for your grants development process and beyond.

- ► **Evaluator Identification:** Locate an evaluator who will agree to work with your organization and your grant programs. If you don't know where to look, a good way to begin is by contacting local colleges or the nearest university branches. The departments that often have strong evaluation programs include sociology, psychology, education, public health, and social work. Further, the faculty in these departments are frequently involved in the evaluation of local programs. Another avenue is to find out who is evaluating existing grants in your geographic area. (We discussed locating grantees in earlier chapters.)

- ► **Evaluator Engagement:** You may need to pay a fee for initial consultative services, but it will be well worth every penny when grants are successful. Oftentimes, evaluation consultants will offer their services during grants planning for free if they are identified in the proposal budget as the consultant to be contracted for program evaluation. (The logistics of contracting consultants will be explained in Step 9.)

► **Evaluation Plans:** Ensure that your grant proposals explain how your program evaluation will be conducted and who will be responsible for it. Consider the basics we have recommended and make sure you have included all relevant components.

►► *Evaluator Independence*

Evaluators are typically contracted by the organization that is administering the grant. It is important that they be independent agents. Even though evaluators are paid for services under the contract, their sole source of income should not be dependent upon either the program being evaluated or the agency administering the program. This autonomy allows the evaluator the freedom to conclude whether or not the program has met with success or failed to achieve its objectives.

For similar reasons, we strongly recommend that employees of the agency receiving a grant not serve as evaluators for the program. Agency employees do not have the freedom to make independent conclusions about program success, or at least they do not appear to have this freedom. Their paycheck depends upon survival of the agency, and this is an implied incentive to declare grant programs successful, regardless of the truth. A better option is to assemble an independent advisory committee to oversee the evaluation, focusing on the committee as the evaluating authority rather than the staff (who may be providing the data).

RA Note: There are exceptions to the recommendation to avoid using employees for project evaluation. These would include smaller grant programs, typically from private sources. Often a foundation that awards a small grant will require only a simple response from the agency regarding allocation of funds and/or services provided. In these cases, it may be a program or agency employee who writes this report.

Evaluation Measures

How Will You Know What You Did?

As discussed in Step 5, program objectives should include achievable ways to assess program success using both quantitative and qualitative evaluation measures. However, even a well-stated objective may not provide the reader with enough information to perceive exactly how the objective will be tracked, measured, and documented. This is the role of the **performance indicator**.

Performance indicators answer the question, How do we know something occurred? It may be helpful to think about a program in the following manner: Suppose that two months after your grant program ended and your former project director moved to another state, you receive a visit from an evaluator or auditor from the funding source. How can you prove that your program actually did something? Can you prove you hired and paid a project director? Yes, you should have personnel and financial records to verify this. Can you prove your task force held regular meetings? Yes, you should have meeting agendas, sign-in sheets, and/or minutes to verify the existence of these meetings. These records would serve as the performance indicators for the objectives or program activities that addressed hiring a project director and providing program oversight via regular task force meetings.

Evaluation measures are known by several mostly interchangeable names. In addition to performance indicators, **indicators of success**, **project milestones**, **benchmarks**, and **measures of success** are all terms commonly used in grant proposals.

Regardless of the type of evaluation you propose for your program, from simple (minutes of a meeting) to complex (statistical comparison of experimental and control groups), your proposal should specify the planned performance indicators. Every program objective in your proposal should have at least one performance indicator associated with it. Often there are several performance indicators that relate to different aspects of the objective. In some proposals the funding source requests that for each program objective the grantwriter identify every discrete program activity that is expected to impact that objective. In this case, of course, each activity would have its own performance indicator(s).

Presenting Evaluation Plans

Clarity Is Critical

Many grantwriters prefer to list the evaluation measures as part of the presentation of program goals and objectives. In this case, whether using paragraph formatting, bulleted lists, or table style, the author would add, for each objective, a descriptive level that specifies the performance indicator. Other grantwriters choose to define measures of evaluation in their description of the program evaluation. And some grant specialists incorporate performance indicators into either program timelines or management plans (which we will explore in Step 8). At Research Associates, we employ whichever presentation technique best fits the RFP and the planned program.

The sample table below, excerpted from a recent Research Associates proposal, illustrates one possible presentation of evaluation measures.

Objectives	Performance Indicators
1. Between 7/1/05 and 6/30/06 establish 5 afterschool centers that will serve at least 100 high-risk students per site in grades PreK-5 (500 total) with a minimum staff-to-student ratio of 1:15.	• Weekly activities log • Student attendance rosters • Site Coordinator screening records for risk status • Verify staff-to-student ratios
2. At least 70% of students will improve academic performance by 10% each year of the grant program.	Year-end grades of students compared to prior year grades annually

►► *Sample Program Evaluation Component*

There are many different techniques available for program evaluation. The sample below, taken from a grant application by Research Associates, is provided for illustrative purposes. This particular sample employs an evaluation methodology developed by Drs. Robert Goodman and Abraham Wandersman and Research Associates. As you read the sample, notice that this proposal explains the use of the evaluation to inform management as well as to determine the success and impact of the program.

The evaluation of the *STARS* project will be a systematic process of collecting, analyzing, and interpreting information to determine the extent to which the objectives and goals of the project have been achieved. The evaluation will determine the level to which the program is effective in meeting the needs of students, their families, the school district, and the community. It will provide information about service delivery that will be useful to program staff and other audiences. The evaluation will be ongoing and will provide feedback to directors, program staff, and the task force to allow for continuing program improvement and to monitor fiscal efficiency.

The evaluation incorporates both quantitative and qualitative examinations of performance, services, and behavior resulting in a judgment concerning program outcomes. The evaluation will include both process and outcome components. Process evaluation provides documentation of the program activities and behavior. It confirms the existence and availability of physical and structural elements of the program and is used to guide planners if modifications are needed in program design. On the other hand, outcome evaluation assesses program achievements and effectiveness in producing favorable cognitive, belief, and behavioral changes.

The leadership of the *STARS* program needs concrete measures of belief or behavior to determine the impact of the program's activities on the lives of its students, parents, teachers, and the community. Input from these four key stakeholders will be collected, analyzed and considered during planning and implementation of the program.

Process Evaluation

Process evaluation serves a dual function. *First*, it is an internal necessity: staff and planners need to know if the project is being implemented as intended, and they need to have this information early enough for any needed corrections to be made. *Second*, process evaluation provides meaning for the outcome evaluation. Outcome evaluation scrutinizes the effects of the program on the population being served. The evaluators for *STARS* will employ the FORECAST model (formative evaluation, consultation, and system techniques) to help guide the project planning and its implementation (Goodman, 1994). The FORECAST system employs four components: models, markers, measures, and meaning.

Models: The Evaluator develops a model of the program exactly as it is presented in the grant proposal in a diagram format so planners and key informants can see all proposed activities illustrated on a flow chart. The Evaluator then meets with the planners to refine the model and ensure everyone understands and agrees with the Evaluator's plans. This collaboration between the evaluation team and planners early in the project implementation prevents later misunderstandings (Wandersman, 1998).

Markers: This model of action is used to develop the markers, which are indicators of project achievement. Markers are key elements for judging whether each element of the project is implemented as rendered in the model of action. Because projects such as *STARS* are complex, program activities may not be implemented exactly as planned. When this happens, there is an increased likelihood that the program will not produce desired outcomes. The Project Director and the Evaluator will work closely in collaboration with planners who will jointly monitor the program to ascertain if the markers are accomplished. The Evaluator will meet monthly with program planners to provide ongoing feedback so mid-course adjustments can be made as needed, increasing the implementation accuracy of the project.

Measures: These provide the details on how the project is to attain each marker and specify data and information to be collected by the staff and the Evaluators. In collaboration with the Project Director, the

Evaluator decides the best way to measure each project marker. The measures will emphasize materials that the program is likely to collect in the course of the implementation such as meeting minutes, reports, telephone logs, staff activity calendars, and project forms. Using materials that are in the process will minimize the data collections burden and enhance staff participation.

Meaning: The final component of the FORECAST model is the determination of the meaning or the criteria used to assess achievement of each marker. Selection of the criteria establishes the minimum level of adequacy of each marker. If the marker is not attained, staff and evaluators have the opportunity to forecast possible consequences and implement solutions to keep the *STARS* project on target. This evaluation model allows for early identification of discrepancies to allow the project to make corrections before any component is compromised.

Outcome Evaluation

Outcome evaluation answers the question, What were the effects of the program? Outcome effects can be short- or long-term. Short-term outcomes measure the effects of the program on the participants, while long-term effects examine the change in the problem(s) or the increase in the positive factors that reduce the problem. The primary goals of the *STARS* project are to: (1) provide a safe, drug-free, and supervised environment for children and their families; (2) deliver an array of services that offer significant expanded learning opportunities for youth and contribute to reduced alcohol abuse and violence; (3) assist students in meeting or exceeding state and local standards in core academic subjects as appropriate to the needs of the children; and (4) work in close collaboration with community organizations and youth development agencies.

▶▶ *Learning more about evaluation.*

Grantwriters who want to learn more about program evaluation have several available options. There are numerous texts, workbooks, and workshops available on this subject. An Internet search on the keyword, "evaluation," yielded a helpful site, **http://gsociology.icaap.org/methods**, that provides links to free resources for evaluation researchers. The links provided are to sites that have information on how to conduct various methods of evaluation and social research.

Another very helpful, resourceful publication is *Measuring Program Outcomes: A Practical Approach* from the United Way of America. This manual was developed with nonprofits in mind and offers a step-by-step approach that is both practical and easy to understand. (To order, call Sales Service/America, a United Way subsidiary, at 1-800-772-0008.)

RA Note: Research Associates offers a three-day seminar in evaluation developed by Jennifer Gouvin, Ph.D. Dr. Gouvin's educational background includes a doctorate from the University of South Carolina in educational psychology and research with an emphasis in evaluation. She was a Fellow Recipient with the Spencer Foundation and has worked as an evaluator, professional development trainer, curriculum designer, and grants consultant with school districts since 1999. Please check the Research Associates website, **www.grantexperts.com**, to learn more about our evaluation seminar and other workshops.

In Closing: In addition to an evaluation plan, there are two other components that may not be required by every funding source but will often add extra points: dissemination of information and program sustainability. The purpose and importance of these components are explained in Step 6.

STEP 7
STRENGTHENING THE PROPOSAL

The good news is that at this point in your program development, you are entering the home stretch. You know the steps for researching the problem and developing program strategies. You have learned how to construct program goal(s) and objectives and to map out an evaluation plan. Now it is time to examine two additional elements of successful grantwriting to strengthen your program and your proposal: disseminating information and project sustainability.

Dissemination of Information
Tooting Your Own Horn!

Dissemination of information is simply telling others about your program—what worked and what did not work. It is the broadcasting of your program findings to audiences who may gain from your experiences. These audiences include not only other grantwriters, professionals, and nonprofits, but also consumers, local leaders, volunteers, key informants, and decision makers.

▶▶ *What is the inherent appeal of dissemination?*

Research Associates recommends including dissemination of information in your grant proposal even if the RFP does not require you to do so. This is primarily because there is an inherent appeal in disseminating information that engages the interest of funding sources. Why an inherent appeal? Because the process of disseminating information provides the grants developer with the opportunity to (1) test a theory on a small or moderately sized group of individuals by implementing and conducting the proposed project; (2) determine what worked and what failed to work by evaluating project outcomes; and (3) aggressively inform others, potentially impacting thousands of individuals. Thus, by using the funder's relatively small investment and creating a ripple effect, the grant program is benefiting many more than the original target population. This is the appeal that serves as a significant selling point to potential funding sources.

An additional plus is that it pleases funders to have their names associated with successful programs broadcast to a larger audience. There are many consumer-oriented foundations (funded by corporations, organizations, and individuals that need and want good publicity). For example, in our community, one company paid for printing all educational materials at our local zoo to associate their name with a favorably perceived project.

▶▶ *Why include dissemination in your proposal?*

In addition to its attractiveness to funding sources, dissemination of information will:

▶ Heighten public awareness about your program and your agency, adding to your reputation as a respected and competent "player" in the local arena.

▶ Potentially benefit future grantwriting and fundraising efforts due to this increased visibility as local decision makers become aware of your track record and program management skills.

▶ Earn extra points from grant reviewers familiar with the potential benefits that dissemination offers to other program planners. *Remember to keep striving for those extra points!*

Where do you incorporate this topic into your proposal? "Dissemination of Information" is an ideal subheading in the Approach, with appropriate chronological placement: **after** you have evaluated your results.

►► *How do you broadcast your findings?*

There are as many ways to tell others about your program findings as there are methods of communicating. While we might stop short of endorsing Morse code, we do encourage creative use of a full range of marketing techniques. *Don't be afraid to toot your own horn!* Here are some ways to do it.

► **Professional Publications:** Develop an article describing your program objectives, implementation experiences, challenges, outcomes, and most importantly, your recommendations for future programs. Such an article offers broad appeal in both the nonprofit and for-profit sectors. Submit it to professional publications in your field and to others that provide similar services or serve the same target population.

► **Conferences:** Presenting workshops at conferences at the local, state, and national levels is always an effective means for sharing program successes and failures. Watch your professional literature for "calls" for presenters or papers and submit a summary of your program results. In addition, many conferences also publish a written version of conference presentations that is made available to a broader audience. (e.g., Internet users).

► **Media Coverage:** Schedule a press conference when you receive a grant award; it's the perfect moment to kick off the new program, publicly applaud your grantwriting team, energize your task force members for the challenges ahead, and notify potential consumers about the new program.

Sometimes you simply have to "create" news to get noticed by the local media. Why not schedule a news conference to announce your program results? Consider inviting several program participants to "tell their stories." Or invite an important community leader such as the mayor to speak at the conference. A news conference will tend to be successful if it features a prepared news release offering program information and results in more detail than will be announced during the conference; a carefully chosen time, such as a "slow" news day (Monday); a convenient location with easy access; an incentive such as refreshments (always a plus); and sufficient advance notice to alert local media and the public.

► **Newspaper Articles:** Don't be deterred if your programs are simply too small to attract media attention; there are other ways to get noticed. Consider drafting an article—or a series of articles—about your program and its results. Keep in mind that you may need a "hook" to attract the attention of a news reporter or editor. An example may be offering to arrange an interview with a program participant, graduate, or impacted family. Of course, editors for small local papers often welcome articles from every source. It also helps to establish and nourish relationships with members of the local media. Send reporters art projects from your program participants to brighten their offices and include an invitation to visit.

► **Newsletters:** You may work with agencies that already produce their own newsletters for distribution. Never miss an opportunity to submit a project update to this publication. Depending on the size and circumstances of your grant project, it may be appropriate to produce and distribute a project newsletter. These vary in size and scope and may be distributed in several manners, not all of which require the expense of postage. For example, a project serving an entire county may produce a brief newsletter for insertion into every electric bill or a tabloid insert for the county newspaper.

► **Internet:** Websites are great places for sharing information about your grant projects. Many existing website offer opportunities for grantees to submit program ideas and recommendations. Your organization or a partnering agency may already have an established website on which you may post this information. Once you have developed a webpage describing your program, be sure you develop as many linkages as possible to increase access to your site and spread the word about your results. Your funding source may also have a website where you can spread the word about your good works. E-mail updates and Listservs are two additional ways to communicate program information that do not incur postage and printing expenses.

➤ **Funder's Publications:** You might also submit news articles to the funding organization for inclusion in its newsletters or other publications. What better way to make friends within the organization than by providing them with an article that creates goodwill? And never underestimate the value of sending a picture of happy program participants. Your program could even make the cover of the funder's next Annual Report! (Of course, always cover your bases by obtaining media release forms from every program participant captured on camera.)

➤ **Public Meetings:** Every community has an established schedule of regular public meetings, such as city or county council meetings. These can be wonderful venues for grants managers to disseminate information to community leaders and the public for minimal investment. And don't overlook local civic organizations. Not only do they include many key informants from your community, they are always looking for speakers and program ideas and they may be an unexpected source of volunteers. Further, these meetings offer wonderful opportunities for establishing credibility for your organization.

RA Secret! Many of the above techniques can be helpful to more than the success of one grant proposal; they may also play a critical role in the continuing viability of your organization. A well-managed agency should establish and maintain strong media relationships. Include a local media person on the advisory committee. Don't wait until your program has ended to tell others what you are doing, but use every opportunity to get the word out.

►► *Disseminate through exportable products.*

Exportable products serve as conduits for disseminating information. They are tangible and usually exist beyond the life of the grant program. Several of the dissemination methods discussed above actually produce tangibles such as the news articles, program updates, and website. There are additional methods for producing exportable products that should be considered in planning for dissemination of your program information. *These strategies may also add points during reviewer scoring!*

► **Create a project manual.** An excellent exportable product is a project manual that explains to others how to run the project. A comprehensive manual should address every component of designing, implementing, carrying out, and evaluating your program. A well-written grant proposal can serve as a good beginning for the manual. A project manual can provide tremendous resources for other program managers and planners.

► **Conduct training.** Taking the concept of the project manual a step further, your organization may decide to offer training opportunities for others interested in conducting similar programs. The training approach may be as low-key as allowing an observer access to your program operations. Observers could "shadow" various team members, (i.e., follow a person around for a day, learning the nuts and bolts of program operations.) Or, you might conduct a formal workshop to present your program structure and operation. Workshop content and materials may be broad in scope, similar to a project manual, providing a complete overview of program operations, or they may have a narrower focus, addressing only selected components of the program. Such workshops can be offered either on-site or in other locations.

► **Produce a curriculum.** Many grant programs, particularly those with prevention objectives or a focus on improving behaviors, will include teaching components. For example, your program for reducing violence may include parenting classes. While some grant programs purchase or utilize existing curricula, others provide for the development of a new or modified curriculum tailored to program objectives and/or the target population. These newly developed curricula are also exportable products.

▶ **Develop a video or DVD.** In today's media-savvy world, a video or DVD is an excellent method for disseminating information. Many of your program components may complement your efforts if you make the effort. For example, the Project Director for an afterschool program worked with fifth-grade students to produce a video with individual "All About Me" segments, written, produced, edited by, and starring each child. This endearing video not only makes a wonderful keepsake for parents but is also a powerful exportable product. The video has been used to successfully engage local businesses and civic groups to offer support for the program and also to encourage other districts to implement similar programs.

▶ **Develop a public service announcement (PSA).** Another approach is the production of a PSA by your project. This concept may be appropriate for your attempts to locate and engage clients for the program or for raising community awareness about community problems you are targeting. Of course, to be successful in obtaining airtime, your PSA should be of professional quality. This is where established partnerships with local television and radio stations can be beneficial. And these partnerships may also benefit your placement in better time slots allotted to public service announcements.

For example, a local nonprofit agency with the mission of education, prevention, intervention, and treatment of substance abuse developed a PSA targeting "boating under the influence" (BUI), a local problem associated with numerous fatalities. The successful campaign raised public awareness of BUI and resulted in a significant reduction in BUI fatalities. As a plus, it also increased agency visibility as a reputable provider of intervention and treatment services.

► **Participate in awards programs.** There are various awards programs in your community, region, and state offered by your professional associations and other organizations. By submitting your project for recognition, you create the opportunity to win an award, thereby spreading the good word about your accomplishments, acknowledging the efforts of program staff and volunteers, and also recognizing the funder who helped you get started.

►► *The secret benefit of disseminating information*

Grantwriters should also recognize the benefits of disseminating information exceed the three primary points discussed thus far: (1) the inherent appeal to funders; (2) the extra points earned from reviewers; and (3) enabling others to learn from your experiences. The "secret" benefit is that both dissemination of information and exportable products can be used to justify both operating expenses and the purchase of equipment for your agency.

As we will discuss in Step 9, the budget should always be program-driven. This means nearly every line item in the budget must clearly relate to at least one program component or activity described in the project narrative. There should be no surprises in the budget. This can be challenging to the grants team who is seeking funding for programs to serve the community as well as for organizational needs. In Step 1 under "Designing a Successful Agency Grants Process," we explained the importance of conducting an organizational needs assessment. Not only must you assess agency needs, you must also occasionally reward the organization and team members with needed equipment and supplies. Dissemination of information offers the grantwriter the opportunity to do so.

There are many items that can be related to—and purchase justified by—the dissemination methods discussed in this section. In other words, by setting the stage programmatically, you can include items (desired by your agency) in your budget to support your program. Let's consider several examples to clarify our point. The list below suggests items that could be justified by each exportable product.

- ► **Articles for Publication:** computers, upgraded word-processing software

- ► **Newsletter Inserts:** publishing software, clip art package, digital camera

- ► **Newsletters:** printers, copiers

- ► **Training:** laptop computer, presentation software, projector, screen

- ► **Conferences:** travel, meeting expenses

- ► **Website:** Internet access, high-speed Internet (DSL) line, computer upgrades

- ► **Video:** camcorder, VCR or DVD burner and/or player

Do not be limited by this list of suggestions; there are other expenses that can be justified in this manner. Also notice that many of the items above may be applied to other categories. For example, a digital camera could be justified by any of the above exportable products.

Wouldn't most agencies be delighted to acquire a few of these items, often referred to as "operating expenses" when taken out of program context? Using our methods, you have developed a creative program that is strongly supported by a program-driven (thus defendable) budget. This grant program and its budget then help the organization by acquiring needed, desirable items for the organization. This is truly a win-win situation!

Program Sustainability

Staying Alive!

One often-troubling aspect of the overall concept of using grants to fund programs is the tendency among many grant programs to simply end when the grant funding expires. This unfortunate trend applies equally to one-year and multiyear programs. Further, this disheartening tendency, which plagues program planners and haunts impacted populations, also disturbs funding sources who are beginning to ask organizations how they plan to sustain the program. For this reason, planning for **program sustainability**, or funding beyond the life of the grant, can be critical in getting your proposal approved for initial funding.

Before we delve into discussing program sustainability, we offer a word of caution. Sustainability is a relatively new term, and your reader may not know it. We advise that you define the concept in your first use of the term, as we did in the paragraph prior to this one ("funding beyond the life of the grant").

Research Associates recommends keeping long-range survival of your program uppermost in your thoughts during program planning and proposal writing. Sustainability is one more component that we urge you to include in your grant proposal, whether or not it is mentioned in the RFP. It will appeal to funding sources and score extra points from reviewers. However, the concept of sustainability may be difficult to comprehend and is often overlooked by planners who are struggling to obtain initial funding.

►► *How do you plan to sustain a dream?*

Grantwriters can address sustainability of their programs by including a project objective or activity aimed at developing a strategic **resource development plan**. Here are several recommendations for developing a successful plan:

► **Produce a written plan.** The benefit of stating that your resource development plan will be written is that in writing it down, you are able to confirm its development and verify its existence. Too often, long-range planning—especially for program income—is an issue that program managers keep "meaning to do" but never quite get around to doing. When there is a program objective to develop a written plan, the development of the plan becomes part of the project management, and program evaluators track its development.

➤ **Identify varied funding sources.** A diversified resource strategy will emphasize varied potential funding sources for continued program operation. For additional grants, these sources are essentially from the same funding pool discussed earlier for original funding in Step 2. Obviously, a diverse plan identifying a combination of government, foundation, and corporate funding sources is stronger than a plan focused on only one funding source.

➤ **Look for diverse funding methods.** Program planners would do well to also consider nongrant methods for institutionalizing a successful program or project component. For example, a program strategy to employ family outreach workers to assist eligible families to apply for and receive public assistance may net sustainable program income in Medicaid dollars.

➤ **Develop short- and long-term strategies.** The resource development plan should identify short-term strategies for additional funding as well as long-range planning for the continued survival of successful program components.

➤ **Focus on success.** Identify program activities that are successful and focus sustainability efforts on them. This crucial activity relates the recommendations of the ongoing evaluation to the efforts of sustainability funding in a positive way.

➤ **Form a sustainability team.** Just as we recommended a grantwriting team for developing your initial proposal, consider forming a team to seek additional funding for program continuation. Select key agency staff, impacted consumers, and community leaders who will be motivated to keep the program operating. If your organization is partnering with other agencies (for this grant program or in other efforts) consider forming an inter-agency grant team. Not only will this collaboration broaden your access to resources, but reviewers will love this concept *(and that means more points)*.

➤ **Train the team.** Be sure to consider providing sufficient funds for the sustainability grants team to attend or receive grants development training. Remember that this item may be included in the budget of the original application if sustainability is an expressed objective of the program.

➤ **Broadcast your success.** As mentioned earlier in this chapter, dissemination of information may play an important role in sustainability. It is important to let community leaders know that your program is making a difference. By increasing public awareness of your agency and this program, you may improve your future funding capability.

In Closing: Your sustainability objective is the development of a **written, diversified resource strategy.** And your goal as the grantwriter is to convince the funding source that your program will survive beyond the initial funding, continuing to provide services to the target population. It is important to begin planning for sustainability early, never waiting until your program is underway. *To achieve sustainability, you begin planning for the end from the beginning!*

In Step 8 we will examine how to develop and write a management plan that placates reviewers and assures funding sources that you possess the necessary management skills to be trustworthy of receiving their grant dollars.

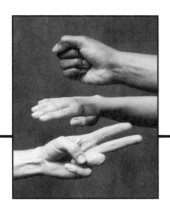

STEP 8
MANAGING THE
PROGRAM

Any strong, well-written grant proposal will explicitly address management planning. A sound **management plan** will chronologically describe the activities or tasks that must occur in the planning, implementation, oversight, and follow-up of your grant project. Research Associates recommends that you include a management plan in most grant proposals. This is important because your ability to describe a competent and effective plan for managing the project will convince funders that you have the requisite management skills to be entrusted with their money.

Management planning for every grant program actually begins when program planners and grantwriters join forces in a collaborative effort to turn their dreams into reality. In fact, each of the steps undertaken in the Research Associates Logical Grantwriting Model is instrumental to the development of a well-planned, achievable project designed to facilitate program oversight and management. The formal process of management planning begins with the establishment of the advisory committee or task force that participates in the proposal planning process (Step 4, "Seven Secrets for a Successful Approach"). You must then project beyond the planning and grantwriting stages of your program. Ask yourself, What will we have to do, step by step, to make this project happen, to make our dreams come true?

Management Planning

Convincing Funders
You Know What You Are Doing!

Management planning for a grant program must address a broader period of time than simply the operation of the project (which normally coincides with the grant's fiscal year). Grants management or oversight encompasses activities conducted during several phases of grants administration. We have differentiated the phases as Planning, Preparation, Start-up, Project Operation, and Follow-Up. As you will see, these phases of program oversight are related to the flow of resources into and out of the administering organization. *Bottom line? Don't spend the grant money before you get it!*

► **Planning:** As we said earlier, management planning begins with the establishment of the advisory committee or grant oversight authority. In most cases, this step has already occurred and the committee or task force has provided input during the proposal planning process.

► **Preparation:** The focus of the management plan then shifts to program start-up details that may be accomplished after the grant award has been announced, but while the organization is still awaiting receipt of grant funds. These activities should require minimal financial resources. Examples include developing job descriptions and preparing employment marketing materials; in-house advertising for grant positions; additional meetings of the advisory committee to review and elaborate program implementation details; and contract negotiations with evaluators and other contracted personnel. *Your agency should protect itself by minimizing financial commitment to the project until the first check arrives (or at least, the letter of award).*

► **Start-up:** The next phase of management oversight addresses activities that incur costs during the first months of the grant's funding period. Start-up activities might include advertising position openings, hiring employees, and engaging clients. We strongly recommend that you plan conservatively by allowing at least two months in the beginning of the project's fiscal year to conduct these start-up activities. In our experience, *it is the rare exception for a new project to begin providing services on day one of project funding—or even in the first sixty days!*

► **Project Operation:** During this phase the program is underway, services are being provided, and you are monitoring progress to make sure the project is on track for meeting objectives. This is the phase when most of your grant money is spent.

► **Follow-up:** The final phase of program oversight involves performing those activities to close down the program if necessary, produce the final evaluation of project outcomes, and then provide the necessary reports for both organizational authorities and funding sources.

We cannot overstate the importance of allowing for a program start-up period. The project cannot begin to provide services until the staff, supplies, and equipment are in place and consumers have been identified and engaged in the program. If you fail to acknowledge the time that these activities will require, you will fall far short of providing the projected number of services. Thus, when the novice grantwriter fails to allow sufficient time for start-up activities, program outcomes are predisposed towards failure!

As you develop your management plan, you will need to determine the degree of detail that is relevant to the project you are proposing. The larger and more complex the program, the greater the detail that is required. A smaller, brief proposal may include only one task for each of the phases prior to and after provision of services.

Good management plans often include a time line that clarifies when each task or activity should occur. Due to the higher volume of necessary service-delivery and oversight activities during the

Project Operation phase, this portion of your management plan is particularly suited to expression via a time line format.

Time Lines

Keeping Your Project on Track

A **time line** indicates when project activities should occur according to planners and helps keep project leaders on task. Once the grant is funded, the time line may need refining, but it is a very handy checklist of what must be accomplished each month.

Project time lines should include administrative and program activities, although the primary focus is on program areas. Tasks are arranged in chronological order, usually by month. Although less common, some RFPs request that time lines be constructed to list tasks by quarter rather than by month.

Most project time lines reflect the fiscal period of the grant program. For many grant programs this is twelve months. For multiyear grants, there are various methods for expressing the time line: (1) listing activities of the first year in detail with a note that subsequent years will follow a similar schedule; (2) listing activities for every month, each year of the project (lengthy); or (3) listing activities for all months in every year of the project but omitting the repeating activities (e.g., a quarterly task force meeting).

Time lines may be presented in a variety of formats including paragraph, bulleted lists, and tables. Whatever the style, you must present the information clearly. For clarity, most time lines should be presented in a tabular format such as the illustration that follows.

This time line is for a generic grant project, meaning that it could apply to a program providing nearly any type of services. The fiscal year is July 2005 through June 2006. (To conserve space, March through June activities are not presented in detail.)

Time Line	
Month	**Program Activities**
July 2005	• Review proposal and design program and budget strategies • Negotiate contracts with program staff and evaluators • Develop oversight plan with evaluators • Meet with staff to identify staff development and training needs • Organize Task Force membership
Aug. 2005	• Hold first Task Force meeting; develop structure for program oversight • Develop detailed job descriptions and personnel ads • Begin advertising for project staff (in-house and external) • Develop necessary forms for documentation and evaluation • Order program equipment and first-quarter supplies
Sept. 2005	• Interview and hire additional project staff • Staff training regarding project mission, protocols, and implementation • Agency outreach workers begin referral of potential clients • Project staff begin contacting and engaging clients
Oct. 2005	• Begin providing program services • Evaluators begin regular monthly site visits
Nov. 2005	• Continue providing program services • Evaluators continue monthly site visits • Quarterly meeting of Task Force; review progress towards objectives • Implement mid-course corrections as needed
Dec. 2005	• Continue providing program services • Evaluators continue monthly site visits
Jan. 2005	• Continue providing program services • Evaluators continue monthly site visits • Sustainability Committee begins regular meeting schedule
Feb. 2005	• Continue providing program services • Evaluators continue monthly site visits • Quarterly meeting of Task Force; review progress towards objectives • Implement mid-course corrections as needed
Mar.–June 2006 *Continue providing program services and evaluating program monthly.*	
July 2005	• Evaluators review project outcomes and prepare Project Summary • Project Director and evaluators prepare Final Reports • Final meeting of Task Force; review Project Summary and Final Reports • Project Reports submitted to Funding Source

Note the clarity achieved by presenting the time line in a table. Also notice how using a bulleted-list style in the Activities column contributes to the clarity.

It is best if the time line fits on one page of the proposal. If this is not possible, you should observe the following: do not allow one month to be split between two pages; do not allow one month to stand alone on a page; and repeat your time line column headings on subsequent pages. Also, whenever a table or other graphic is inserted into your grant proposal, the paragraph preceding it should introduce its purpose.

Remember that a table allows you to pack more information into less space because tables are generally accepted in a single-spaced format. This is important when the RFP requires you to use double spacing and the project narrative is constrained in length.

Our sample time line is a simple one. It omits recommended proposal components such as dissemination of information and does not mention sustainability until the seventh month. Also, because it is generic, the program services are not described in detail.

On the other hand, the time line does provide a fairly thorough review of administrative activities during the pre-start-up and start-up phases. Many of these are similar regardless of the type of project that you are implementing. Depending upon your grant application or RFP and your approach to describing your management plan, the time line may be more heavily focused on program tasks with few administrative tasks included.

Additional items worth noting in the time line include:

► **Duration:** Despite the fact that the funding is for a twelve-month period, the time line encompasses thirteen months; the last month is restricted to follow-up activities only (program services and funding have ceased).

► **Beginning of Services:** The first two months address administrative tasks only; the first program services would be the referral, contact, and engagement of consumers or clients in the third month.

► **Saving Space:** If length of the program narrative is a problem in your proposal, several of the tasks shown could be eliminated to conserve space. For example, it is not really necessary to include "Continue providing program services," for once you have begun them, their continuation is implied. The same applies to the evaluation visits.

Presenting the Management Plan

Trust Us, It Can Be Simple!

If you are feeling overwhelmed by the prospect of attempting to describe your management plan comprehensively and clearly, do not despair. This can be accomplished simply. Begin with a time line table that has columns for Date and Activity. Add a column that identifies "Person Responsible." *Voila!* You have a management plan!

Our only caution about this method is to be sure your management plan includes both administrative and service-delivery components. Because it is simpler to identify the tangible elements of delivering services, the necessary administrative and evaluative tasks are often overlooked. You might consider arranging a special review of your management plan by a grantwriting team member with excellent attention to detail *(your obsessive-compulsive team member works well here).* Seriously, take whatever steps are necessary to be sure your plan includes all tasks identified by planners and evaluators as important to project implementation and oversight.

►► *Simple Management Plan Presentation*

To illustrate this method of presenting the management plan, the sample that follows was excerpted from the generic time line sample, but includes only August and September. Your management plan must encompass the project fiscal year or the entire length of your program.

Management Plan		
Month	**Activities**	**Person Responsible**
Aug. 2005	First Task Force meeting; develop structure for program oversight	Agency Director, Evaluators
	Develop detailed job descriptions and personnel ads	Agency Director
	Begin advertising for project staff (in-house and external)	Agency Director
	Interview and hire Project Director	Task Force
	Develop necessary forms for documentation and evaluation	Project Director, Evaluators
	Order program equipment and first-quarter supplies	Project Director
Sept. 2005	Interview and hire additional project staff	Project Director
	Staff training regarding project mission, protocols, and implementation	Project Director
	Agency outreach workers begin referral of potential clients	Project Director
	Project staff begin contacting and engaging clients	Project Director

Notice that in this table, instead of presenting activities in a bulleted list, a row is allocated for each activity. This makes it easy to assign responsibility for the task.

RA Tip! Always make sure your tables are clear and easy to comprehend. *Your score will suffer when reviewers are confused and irritated.*

►► *Adding Evaluation Components*

As we have emphasized, quality management planning includes not only administration, program implementation, and service-delivery tasks, it also addresses the related efforts of evaluation and ongoing oversight of the project. Taking our management plan one step further, we suggest adding a fourth column for "Performance Indicator." *Voila!* You have an Evaluation Plan! Grantwriting doesn't have to be complicated; it just takes planning and some attention to detail.

The abbreviated table below presents one method for succinctly presenting a management plan with evaluative components.

Management Plan			
Date	**Activities**	**Person Responsible**	**Performance Indicator**
Aug. 2005	First Task Force meeting; develop structure for program oversight	Agency Director, Evaluators	Meeting minutes
	Develop detailed job descriptions and personnel ads	Agency Director	Personnel records
	Begin advertising for project staff (in-house and external)	Agency Director	Personnel records
	Interview and hire Project Director	Task Force	Personnel records
	Develop necessary forms for documentation and evaluation	Project Director, Evaluators	Forms
	Order program equipment and first-quarter supplies	Project Director	Fiscal record
Sept. 2005	Interview and hire additional project staff	Project Director	Personnel records
	Staff training regarding project mission, protocols, and implementation	Project Director	Meeting minutes
	Agency outreach workers begin referral of potential clients	Project Director	Referral logs
	Project staff begin contacting and engaging clients	Project Director	Service logs, Client Records

Relating Project Tasks to Program Goals

Tying It All Together

RFPs or grant applications sometimes require proposal writers to demonstrate the relationship between each project activity and the program goals and objectives. This requirement is valid, for it ensures that all project activities are relevant and focused on the goals of the program. Since our approach to expressing program goals and objectives has generally been to relate one or more objectives to each program goal, we will now show how to link each task or activity to its corresponding project objective, which will connect it as well to the appropriate program goal.

As in many things, there is more than one way to demonstrate this relationship in your grant proposal. Grantwriters commonly employ one of two methods:

►► *Focus on objectives.*

Using this method, the writer states (or re-states) each program objective followed by the related project tasks or activities. For each objective, you could go a step further and include additional information such as beginning date, person responsible, or performance indicator for each task. Again, we would recommend presenting this information in a table to minimize confusion.

Caution: Once when we used this approach, our table included columns for Objective, Activities, Date, and Performance Indicator. One of the RFP requirements was a project time line. Since our table already included a date for each activity, we thought that we had provided a time line. However, we received a call during the review process with the question, Why did you fail to include a time line? Ouch! Our advice from this experience is to consider the second presentation method if your reviewers will be looking for a separate time line.

▶▶ Focus on activities.

In this method, the writer begins by stating each project activity and then indicates the objective(s) this activity will address. As in the first method, additional information may be included for clarification; a tabular format is also recommended.

There are several of advantages to this method. First, there are situations in which one program activity may address several program objectives. This relationship can be easily conveyed with this approach. A second advantage is that this approach can be a space-saver. This is because in the first method, each objective is usually stated in its entirety. With an activity focus, the appropriate objective(s) may be referenced by number if they have been so numbered in the application.

It is simple to arrange a table so that the first column provides date, followed by columns for activity and then objective. Had we done this (in our caution example above), we would have shown the relationship between project tasks and program objectives while also clearly presenting a project time line.

In Closing: We have provided you with a solid yet simple technique for developing your management plan and showed you how to present this plan. This completes the development and description of a proposed project. Step 9 will address how to develop a program-driven budget.

STEP 9
BUILDING THE
BUDGET

We know many of you think budgets are boring and want to skip this chapter. Or some of you are terrified at the thought of trying to develop a program budget. Or worse, you just want to let someone else "figure it out." Stick with us. You can do it, and it is important to the success of your grant proposal that **you** take the lead in building your proposal budget. To become a successful grantwriter, you really need to know how to construct a program-driven budget.

When all is said and done, the most important factor in developing a successful grant proposal is remembering that *the program drives the budget, and not vice versa.* Grants are awarded to planners who develop creative programs to make the world a better place. They are rarely awarded to planners who are trying to buy things for their agencies or even to those simply trying to keep their doors open. Although you may know what you need to purchase before you put the first word of the proposal on paper, the reviewer must see that the problem drives the program, and the program drives the budget. Funders are interested in making things happen; they, too, want to make the world a better place. You are their vehicle for change by building the bus; the budget simply pays for the gas. Your budget **must** be program-driven.

At Research Associates, we believe one of the primary reasons for our grants success rate is the manner in which we present program budgets in our grant proposals. We integrate information from the program narrative and also include formula components for nearly every line-item entry; consequently, it is rare for our grant budgets to be reduced. This line-item justification is integral to our success because not only must the program drive the budget, the budget must also stand alone. This is because the budget analyst often does not read the program narrative and may not understand why a particular line item is needed.

Most grant budgets reflect costs that may be allocated to one of three categories:

► **Direct Costs:** These are the monies the grant proposal requests from the funding source.

► **Local In-kind or Cash Contributions:** These are services, goods, and cash being donated to the grant program by the local partners; for example, free use of a meeting room.

► **Indirect Costs:** These are the costs associated with operating a program and are typically administrative and not reimbursed; for example, processing payroll.

In fact, the real cost of operating a grant program is the sum total of the direct costs, indirect costs, and local contributions.

In this chapter we take a closer look at what the grantwriter needs to consider when developing appropriate estimated costs for these typical grant budget categories. The word "appropriate" is important because budget analysts who review grant budgets tend to be very familiar with actual program operating costs in the real world. Thus, it is important for your cost estimates to be reality-based and also clearly related to program operation.

Direct Costs
It's Going to Cost How Much?

For the most part, the **direct costs** of your program are those monies you request from the funding source in your grant proposal.

Typically, these are the operating expenses of the program: the standard line-item budget categories found in most program operating budgets. There may be slight variations, however, in the terms used to describe each category.

At Research Associates, we recommend that most grant budgets include the following categories: **Personnel, Fringe Benefits, Travel, Equipment, Supplies, Contractual, Other,** and **Total**. These are the same terms used in the standard Federal Budget Information Form (Form No. 524). Of course, if your RFP provides a different budget format, supplies a budget form, or suggests differently worded entries for budget line items, you should follow their recommendation. *We are still keeping those reviewers happy.*

Let's examine what the grantwriter needs to consider when estimating costs for these grant budget categories. *Remember, the proposed budget is only a guide or plan for spending grant monies. You can change this later, if necessary.*

▶▶ *Personnel*

Personnel includes the salaries of all staff that will be employed by or paid with grant funds. It is important to place only salaried staff under Personnel; contracted staff and consultants (who are technically not employees) go under Contractual or Contracted Services. Salaried staff includes full-time and part-time employees.

Since grant programs are typically built around providing services to a target population, Personnel is nearly always the largest item in any grant budget. It is important to your program's success that you attract qualified staff and important to your proposal's success that your salary ranges be appropriate and reasonable.

So as the grantwriter, sitting alone in your office, you have to estimate the cost of salaries for employees your agency has never employed. Where do you begin? We have several recommendations to assist you.

➤ **Ask others in your agency.** If you work within a large organization, you may have the luxury of simply contacting the personnel office. They should have a good handle on the local employment scene and can assist with your salary estimations. Even if your program is small, your personnel manager, finance officer, or agency administrator should be able to guide you in estimating salary ranges.

➤ **Search the web.** An excellent resource is located at **www.salary.com**. This website offers national salary surveys, trends, calculations for salaries in fifteen different industries, and much more.

➤ **Check with similar programs in your community.** Try communicating with other service providers in the area to get a feel for the salary range needed to attract competent staff locally. Even if your project strategies are creative and new, chances are there are programs in your community—or at least nearby—that offer services similar in nature. Plus, it always helps to know what the competition is paying.

➤ **Compare state and national salary statistics.** Sources such as the U.S. Department of Labor and your state labor department provide information about salary ranges for various classifications of jobs. These statistics can be a good starting place if you have no other basis for comparison. Your local Chamber of Commerce will also have information on salary ranges in the private business and nonprofit sectors.

➤ **Focus on the middle.** As you gather information, you should be able to determine a range of salaries for each staff position or level of staffing in your grant program. Your best strategy is to allocate grant salaries in the median area of this range. *Not too hot, not too cold, but just right!*

➤ **Account for the "soft" money factor.** Having recommended that you focus your salary estimates on a median range, we now offer one disclaimer: Keep in mind that jobs funded by grant programs are paid by "soft" money, or money that typically goes away when the project ends in one, three, or five years. Because qualified personnel may be more attracted to permanent positions, you may have to offer higher salaries to compensate for hiring with soft or grant money. When compensating for this soft-money factor, you should consider the local job market and the legitimate possibilities of continuing the project when the grant funding ends.

► **Sometimes, you just have to guess.** *Enough said.*

Personnel is one budget category that offers flexibility to program planners because it is affected by a factor that impacts estimated totals. This factor is the **prorating** of salaries (adjusting salary cost estimates for employees who do not work the entire fiscal year of the project). Remember in our discussion of management planning in Step 8, we recommended allowing a minimum two-month start-up time for any new grant program. It will generally take two months to advertise, interview, and hire project staff. This delay will impact annual staff salaries during your first program year, and you should adjust your cost estimates to allow for this.

Let's consider an example. Suppose you plan to hire two outreach workers at an annual salary of $18,000 each. You project they will start work the third month of your project. To estimate the cost for the workers, the calculation is: 2 (employees) x $18,000 (annual salary) x 10/12 (pro-rated for 10 months) for a total of $30,000. In the Personnel category of your budget, the line item, Outreach Workers (in the column for Year 1) is $30,000.

There are several questions to consider when deciding whether to prorate annual salaries in your grant budget.

► **Should you prorate salaries for all employees?** No. Obviously, your project planning may bring different employees on board at different times. The most common exception is your Project Director, who nearly always should be hired early in the program to assist in management planning and the hiring of other staff.

► **Should you always prorate salaries to allow for start-up?** No. Every program does not require start-up periods. For example, an agency already operating a similar program with personnel in place may implement a grant program that, although new, is replacing an existing grant program that is phasing out.

► **What if reviewers become confused?** One problem that may occur is that the reviewer may glance at a salary prorated in one year and then erroneously conclude that the increase in the next fiscal year is due solely to a salary increase. Obviously, the reviewer will question your program planning skills (or your math abilities).

This misunderstanding has happened to us. We have received inquiries from reviewers who were shocked because they thought we were awarding excessive raises in salary. Even though we explained the prorating, the reviewers were not happy; their hackles had been raised. They did not trust our management skills, and our reviewer scores dropped.

Therefore, if you choose to prorate salaries, you must ensure that the budget narrative and any formulas clearly indicate the effects of the prorating.

For programs seeking multiple-year funding, one other factor will impact Personnel totals: **inflation**. Because the cost of living tends to rise at a regular rate, we recommend planning for a 5-percent increase in salary for each subsequent program year. In our experience, even programs that discourage or disallow additional program costs in subsequent years will generally approve simple cost-of-living salary increases in the budget.

The table that follows illustrates a sample Personnel budget. Note the explanation of the prorated line item (IB) and the 5-percent "across-the-board" inflation increase reflected in Year 2 estimates.

Budget Category	Year 1	Year 2	Project Total
I. PERSONNEL			
A. Project Director. Full-time Project Director to oversee the grant program, with master's degree and relevant program experience.	$35,000	$36,750	$71,750
B. Outreach Workers. 2 workers @ $18,000 each. Salary is prorated over 10 months in Year 1 as workers will not be hired until Month 3 of the program.	30,000	37,800	67,800
Subtotal Personnel	**$65,000**	**$74,550**	**$139,550**

RA Secret! Before leaving Personnel, we offer another tip for creating successful proposals. Any proposal that includes a full-time employee in the budget should also provide a job description for the position, usually in an appendix.

This brings up the question of job description versus *curriculum vitae*. Some grantwriters routinely include the *curriculum vitae* for personnel identified for employment in their grant applications. However, unless the RFP specifically requests *curriculum vitae,* we recommend including only the more generic job description. This preference serves several purposes: (1) it avoids linking the project to the reputation and capabilities of specific individuals; (2) it avoids the problem of having to seek the approval of the funding source before hiring necessary replacement personnel; and (3) it reduces the tendency of some funding sources to micro-manage a project. (If you would like assistance in developing job descriptions, consider the Research Associates Directory of Job Descriptions on CD that contains more than 75 job descriptions commonly used in grant programs.)

▶▶ *Fringe Benefits*

Fringe Benefits are the taxes and other benefits that employers are required to pay for every employee. These include Social Security (FICA), Federal and State Unemployment Taxes and Unemployment Insurance (FUTA and SUTA), and Workers' Compensation. There are also additional benefits that employers routinely provide, some of which are not required by law. These may include medical, dental, disability, and life insurance; paid sick and annual leave; and retirement benefits.

The cost of Fringe Benefits is based primarily upon gross salaries. The rate varies according to the state and the practices of individual organizations but averages about 21 percent for private nonprofits and 25 to 30 percent for most other agencies. We recommend that you target 25 to 27 percent of total gross salaries to estimate Fringe Benefits for most grant proposals.

RA Warning: Some reviewers will not know that Fringe Benefits exist or that they are required by law. They may then erroneously conclude that you are planning to somehow "benefit" employees with additional salary. For this reason, we recommend that in your budget, you explain and justify the entry for Fringe Benefits with a statement indicating that these benefits are "required by federal and state law."

The table that follows extends our Personnel example and includes a minimal Fringe Benefits explanation. You may elect to explain Fringe Benefits in more detail than the sample below by listing each individual item included in your agency's benefits package. Again, your finance office or bookkeeper should be able to provide this information for you.

Budget Category	Total
I. PERSONNEL	
A. Project Director. Full-time Project Director to oversee the grant program, with Master's degree and relevant program experience.	$35,000
B. Outreach Workers. 2 workers @ $18,000 each. Salary is prorated over 10 months in Year 1 as workers will not be hired until Month 3 of the program.	30,000
Subtotal Personnel	**$65,000**
II. FRINGE BENEFITS	
Standard fringe benefits package, as required by federal and state law, calculated at 25% of gross salaries.	16,250
Subtotal Fringe Benefits	**$16,250**

►► *Travel*

Obviously, Travel budgets provide for costs associated with employee travel and transportation. Less obvious and often overlooked by grantwriters is that transportation for the target population is also a valid Travel item. Travel costs can be the most difficult for planners to estimate and are often the most frequently questioned during grants review. In fact, Travel budgets tend to be heavily scrutinized by reviewers. We believe that this occurs for several reasons, and it may help you plan better if you understand them.

► **Jealousy:** When agencies undergo a budget squeeze, often the first item that is reduced or eliminated is Travel. Thus, your proposal may be reviewed by someone who has lost travel benefits at some time. *If they can't travel, why should you?*

► **Luxury:** There is a widely accepted perception that traveling is a luxury item. This may stem from the tendency for agencies to restrict travel first when money is tight; after all, if it is not a necessity, it must be frivolous. *However, those of us who travel to workshops to teach grantwriting might disagree; travel is hard work and often necessary.*

➤ **Distrust:** Due to the nature of the grants process, once a Travel budget is approved, most grantees are free to use the money however they wish, as long as it is still spent for relevant travel. *Reviewers may worry that your employees will not actually attend all-day working conferences in your state capitol and might instead tour the local sights.*

From our sometimes-painful experiences, Research Associates offers a few pointers that will improve the chances of having your Travel line items approved.

➤ **Explain why travel is required.** It is critical that you explain the reason for any travel item. This can downplay the notion that travel is a luxury and unnecessary. We were once asked by reviewers, Why is it necessary for your Project Director to go to Washington, DC? We could hardly believe our ears! The RFP required every Project Director to attend an annual national meeting in Washington. Since that experience, we always indicate the reason for travel; for example, "As required by the funding source and outlined in the RFP, the Project Director will attend the National Conference in Washington, DC."

➤ **Provide detailed formulas.** Despite the fact many of your projections for travel are, at best, "guesstimates," you still need to provide the items and formulas you used to devise your estimate. For example, for a conference you should include each of the following that apply: conference registration fees; air fare, airport parking fees, ground transportation in the destination city, or reimbursement for mileage in a personal automobile; hotel rates and per diem for food; and number of days of travel. *Just imagine traveling to a workshop and think about each step of your journey.*

➤ **Avoid using round numbers.** If you arrive at a conveniently round number such as $1,000, the reviewers will know you are guessing. You might still be guessing, but provide some detail and the formula. Make your total appear honest by landing on an odd number such as $987.

➤ **Use realistic, but conservative, numbers.** Again, we advise you to keep in mind that most budget reviewers do "live in the real world" and have a pretty good idea of what things cost. A good place to start is with the travel allowances established for state agencies or other nonprofits. Ask similar agencies for their travel policies and rate schedules. If for some reason, your travel costs are higher than average, be sure you document this reason. For example, agencies located in geographically larger states such as Alaska and Texas might incur higher travel costs to attend statewide meetings. And while you might respond "Duh!," we would recommend you mention this increased distance in the travel budget; the reviewer might not otherwise understand the higher estimates without explanation. *Continue to spoonfeed the reviewer.*

RA Secret! Our last recommendation for Travel budgets is an important Research Associates secret because implementing this technique has basically eliminated queries about our Travel budgets. It is a simple maneuver: break your Project Travel into subcategories. Think about it: your travel plans may include national travel, in-state travel, and local travel for employees and also transportation for clients on both a regular basis and for special circumstances. Breaking these into subcategories impacts the perception of the reviewer, even though the subtotal for all Travel remains the same.

The table that follows illustrates the Travel portion of a sample generic grant budget requesting one year of funding. The descriptions provided are to stimulate your thinking about items that might be appropriate for your Travel budget.

Budget Category	Total
III. TRAVEL	
A. National Travel. As required by funding source, the Project Director will attend the National Conference in Washington, DC. Air fare ($475) + ground transportation to/from airport ($50) + 3 hotel nights @ $110 per night including taxes ($330) + per diem for meals @ $35 x 3 days ($105).	$960
B. In-state Travel. For several relevant day-long seminars offered at no charge in the state capitol; 8 trips x (lunch @ $12.50 + 150 miles per round trip @ $0.38 per mile).	556
C. Local Travel. Two outreach workers will use their personal automobiles to travel to client homes and attend relevant community meetings. Estimated 90 miles per week @ $0.38 per mile x 48 weeks average travel (excludes sick/annual/holiday leaves) x 2 staff.	3,283
D. Client Transportation. Consumers must be transported to central services site 2 days per week. 2 days per week x 40 weeks (projected program length) x 2 bus round-trips per day (50 clients per trip for 100 clients total) x 75 miles per trip @ $0.96 per mile (per bus).	11,520
E. Educational Field Trips. Client trips are planned 4 times per year x 2 buses (50 clients per bus) x 100 miles each @ $0.96 per mile (per bus).	768
Subtotal Travel	**$17,087**

▶▶ *Equipment*

The Equipment category includes "big ticket" items in your grant proposal such as computers and large copiers. Equipment items generally cost more than items in the Supplies category. Typically, organizations treat equipment differently than supplies by (a) tagging and tracking equipment via an inventory control system, and (b) depreciating equipment in the annual accounting. However, these practices vary among organizations.

As a rule, funding sources define somewhere in the RFP the amount an item must cost to qualify as equipment. Some organizations define this cut-off point as low as $50, while others may establish it at $5,000 or higher. Your budget plan should reflect the differentiation quoted in the RFP; if the RFP fails to provide one, then rely on the definition utilized by your organization's finance office.

> A few years ago, there was a federal grant RFP in which Equipment purchases were not allowed but Supplies could cost up to $20,000. One grant proposal from a creative grantwriter acquired sorely needed program transportation by purchasing a van as a Supply line item because it cost less than $20,000! Can you believe it? It is true.

The grantwriter's decision to include Equipment in the program budget must be made carefully because funding sources are often suspicious of equipment purchases. Following the suggestions below will improve your chances for getting equipment requests approved by budget analysts.

➤ **Document the programmatic need.** Continuing our theme of a program-driven budget, any equipment purchases absolutely must tie in to program needs. Due to the increased scrutiny of equipment purchases, it is imperative that your line-item description for every item under Equipment express the item's relevance to the program. For examples of suggested wording, review the sample budget excerpt below.

➤ **Avoid specific name brands or models.** It is a generally accepted "no-no" to request a particular piece of equipment by brand name or by model in a grant budget. Your description must be generic (unless it is an equipment grant), allowing for products from several companies to be considered. If, in fact, you have a specific brand in mind as you draft your equipment description, simply omit the brand name. With computers and other technical equipment, it is acceptable to specify that the item be compatible with a brand name. For example, the budget segment below includes an "IBM-compatible" computer. Also consider adding the phrase "by bid process" to show that you are a responsible manager of funds who will seek the best price for your equipment.

► **Provide equipment specifications.** Each equipment request should be thoroughly defined, including all relevant technical and physical specifications. This suggestion offers a level of protection to the grantee, particularly since the use of brand names is discouraged. It also shows you've done your research homework.

The table below presents the Equipment category portion of a sample grant budget requesting one year of funding. The descriptions offer wording addressing the guidelines above.

Budget Category	Total
IV. EQUIPMENT	
A. Computer Technology. IBM-compatible 2.5 GHz computer with 512 MB of RAM; high-resolution 19" color monitor; 80 GB hard drive; 3.5" diskette drive; 750 MB zip drive; 48X DVD-ROM; 56K-90v modem; and 64 MB graphics card. Equipment will be used to develop brochures, newsletters, and flyers about our services. It will also be used to create documents, store evaluation data required by the funding source, and maintain service information for each client. Cost estimate includes sales tax, 3-year warranty, and shipping.	$1,258
B. High-Speed Copier System. Will copy 50 pages per minute and have a 1,000-page bin, 20-page collator, reduction/enlarger feature, stapler, and one-year warranty. Needed to reproduce reports for 13 committees, 6 staff members, and 10 volunteers. Will be used to reproduce flyers, public awareness reports, committee documents, client files, staff minutes, and for general support.	9,890
Subtotal Equipment	**$11,148**

►► *Supplies*

Both the administrative and service-delivery components of your project will require Supplies. As previously discussed under Equipment, the typical RFP will define the difference between the Equipment and Supplies categories according to the funding source. General Office Supplies should be included in almost any type of grant program; additional subcategories will reflect the types of services your program plans to provide.

The table below shows a sample Supplies portion from an actual Research Associates grant budget for an afterschool program. Notice the inclusion of a formula to justify the cost estimates.

Budget Category	Total
V. SUPPLIES	
A. General Office Supplies. Cost estimated at $50 per month x 3 employees x 12 months (includes supplies such as paper, pens, tape, etc.).	$1,800
B. Educational/Training Supplies. Cost estimated at $150 per month x 2 employees x 12 months (includes educational items such as curricula, training notebooks, classroom handouts, etc.).	3,600
C. Computer Supplies. Cost estimated at $100 per month per computer x 2 computer/laser systems x 12 months (includes high-density laser toner cartridges at $90 each, anti-static materials, disks, laser paper, cleaner, etc.).	2,400
D. Nutritional Food Supplies. Cost estimated at $0.65 per student per day x 50 students x 4 days per week x 30 weeks. Students will require a nutritional snack upon arrival to boost energy levels and supplement vitamin intake.	3,900
Subtotal Supplies	**$11,700**

RA Tip! The Supplies category of the budget yields fertile ground for more grantwriting tips.

➤ **Office Supply Limits:** It has been our experience that most budget analysts will approve up to $50 per month per employee in the grant for "general office supplies." (At a minimum, this holds true for full-time administrative employees; inclusion of others would depend upon their job descriptions.)

➤ **"Technology" Appeals:** Wording in both the program narrative and the budget description can be critical to the approval of Supplies items. For example, don't request a computer; instead request "computer technology." And rather than a video camera, ask for "video technology" in your program description.

➤ **Careful Wording:** Notice that Supply item D in the previous table is a request for "nutritional" food supplies rather than a "snack." Sometimes, it is all in the wording!

►► *Contractual*

Contractual work is any service that requires a contract, written agreement, or verbal agreement to be implemented. It is best defined as a service or product. Typically, the agency has very limited control over how the product is developed but does approve the end product. Contractual line items in a grant program might include contracted personnel providing professional or expert consulting services (e.g., training or evaluation), vendors providing access to technology (e.g., Internet access), or leased services (e.g., telephone service). The Contractual or Contracted Services category is also referred to as Purchased Services by some funders.

It may be difficult to determine whether certain personnel should be considered as salaried employees or contractors, and the novice grantwriter often struggles with this issue. (In Research Associates' Certified Grants Administrator Seminar, we review the seventeen rules to define salaried versus contracted personnel.) The following guidelines will assist in this determination:

➤ The agency neither dictates nor defines the hours that the contractor works.

► The agency does not generally provide office space for the contractor (i.e., the worker is not on site on a regular basis).

► The agency does not pay fringe benefits for the contractor.

The bottom line? If the agency controls the hours or provides office space, then the worker is typically considered salaried personnel.

The table below shows a Contractual category from a grant budget. This example has one contract for services and two for contracted personnel.

Budget Category	Total
VI. CONTRACTUAL	
A. Internet Access. Contract with local provider for Internet access for project administrators (required by the RFP for project reporting and ongoing communication with funding source) at a cost of $40 per month x 12 months.	$480
B. Technical Assistance. Professionals from identified model grant program will provide technical assistance and consultation to each site at a cost of $400 per day x 2 consultants x estimated 9 days in Year 1.	7,200
C. Evaluation and Consultation. The Evaluation Group, a university-affiliated organization with 20 years' experience, will provide process and outcome evaluation for this program. Expenses include consultant fees for 5 evaluators, a statistician, and research assistants. Program evaluation was recommended in the RFP. Evaluation contract reflects 9% of program total, significantly lower than the standard evaluation recommendation of 12 to 15% . The Evaluation Group will also provide ongoing management and program and technical assistance to deliver services and consultation that staff cannot provide.	14,996
Subtotal Contractual	**$22,676**

RA Note: A grant proposal that includes contracted personnel may benefit from including a consultant job description in an appendix.

This can be particularly helpful in clarifying both the role of and the necessity for an identified consultant in the grant proposal. A sample description follows.

Consultant Job Description

Duties and Responsibilities:

- Develop contracts required by the grant with various agencies, evaluators, and consultants.

- Assist in project start-up activities such as writing job descriptions, conducting interviews, convening the community task force, etc.

- Serve as an independent professional, screening applicants and providing feedback to staff and community leaders during the hiring of the Project Director.

- Assist in the design of a project management system that is efficient and effective.

- Provide consulting services in the procurement of computers (including needs assessment, recommendation for system design, and securing competitive bids).

- Work with the Project Director and planning committee to maintain momentum, enthusiasm, and commitment to the project.

- Design and implement a comprehensive public awareness campaign that delivers a positive image of the project to the local community.

- Serve as a problem solver for staff, community members, and planning groups.

- Assist in the design of a resource development plan to extend funding of program activities beyond the final year of grant funding.

- Work with local businesses to attract their participation and in-kind services.

- Assist in financial analysis of budget expenses with staff.

- Conduct training needs assessment and coordinate training events.

▶▶ *Other*

The last category in most budgets is Other and includes exactly that: all other items that do not fit into the previously discussed categories. Although Other is typically a "catch-all" category, we nevertheless recommend that the subtotal cost estimate for this category remain relatively low compared to other subtotals; you don't want to raise a red flag here.

There is no way to provide a simple list of items that might be included in Other, as the possibilities are truly endless. It is the category of default for any budget line items **not** appropriate for Personnel, Fringe Benefits, Travel, Equipment, Supplies, or Contractual.

The table below presents a sample Other category for a grant budget.

Budget Category	Total
VII. OTHER	
A. Postage. Required for correspondence, appointment reminders, and newsletters to agency partners, clients, and volunteers at an estimated cost of $110 per month x 12 months.	$1,320
B. Liability Insurance. Policy provides liability protection for treatment professionals and general liability for accidents at program sites. This cost is an amendment to our existing policy (which is awarded via a bid process).	995
C. Employment Advertising. Advertising for 5 administrative staff positions. Cost estimated at $75 per ad x 3 major metropolitan newspapers x 2 Sunday editions.	1,450
Subtotal Other	**$3,765**

▶▶ *Wrapping Up Direct Expenses*

In closing our discussion of the direct expense budget categories, we offer one additional insight. When your grant proposal is approved and you receive that coveted Letter of Award, you will also receive specific instructions regarding your spending guidelines and limits from the funding source. Although individual funding sources do vary, most grants allow funds to be shifted **within** a budget category without prior approval and without penalty. This means, for example, that you could shift funds between those subcategory line items that you created in your travel budget as needed (if your client transportation costs increased, then you could decrease field trips or staff conferences).

This concept is important not only to grant managers but also to grant planners. We recommend that the grantwriter review the total budget, considering this flexibility factor against the probability of implementation problems in various program components.

In recent years, there has been a trend toward even more leniency in budget management at the federal level. For example, in many current grants, the U.S. Department of Education now allows transfer of funds from one budget category to another without prior approval if the "scope of program services" is not changed. This relaxed approach is a wonderful benefit to program managers, allowing them the flexibility to adjust programs to deal with the unexpected in a timely fashion. A word of caution here, however: don't forget to document any fund transfers. In case of an audit, you will be glad you kept track of all financial activity.

In-Kind Contributions
Proving the Community Cares

In-kind contributions include all goods and services that are donated to a project at no cost. They may be donated by the community and by the administering agency. Because these contributions demonstrate both community and agency support for the project, they are a strong selling point to many funding sources. In-kind donations tend to impress both budget analysts and reviewers as evidence that the program will be favorably received and supported at the local level.

There is no limit to the scope of possible goods or services that can be donated to a project. Program planners and grantwriters are limited only by a lack of creative thinking skills! There are some basic items that could apply to almost any grant program, particularly for contributions from the administering agency. These would include the use of the agency's office space, office furniture, utilities, janitorial services, existing telephones, etc. Of course, these would apply only if the agency is planning to actually "house" (or provide office space for) staff in existing agency facilities.

Donations from the community encompass a wide spectrum of possibilities. They might include the donation of facilities for committee meetings or provision of services by local faith-based organizations, libraries, Chambers of Commerce, hotels, or other groups; donated advertising for public awareness or program hiring by print and broadcast media; donated refreshments for various program events from local grocery stores and restaurants; and volunteer manpower from every possible source.

The value of the donated goods or services should be estimated based on their fair market value. In other words, what would it cost the program to purchase this good or service? For most items, these values are relatively simple to obtain. However, estimating the value of volunteer hours can be a challenge.

▶▶ *The Value of Volunteers*

One of the best assets that a community can offer your program is the time provided by volunteers. Unfortunately, many novice grantwriters and program planners fail to recognize the impact of this contribution during budget preparation. Sometimes this is because the grantwriter is unable to estimate the value of this contribution.

Fortunately for grantwriters, the organization, **Independent Sector**, tracks data concerning giving and volunteering in the United States. Their information includes the calculation of an accepted estimate for the hourly value of volunteer time. The value of a volunteer hour has steadily increased from $7.46 in 1980 to $17.19 in 2003. We recommend visiting the Independent Sector website at **www.independentsector.org** for the latest value.

One caution about the calculation of volunteer time: If your project volunteer is a professional and the services provided are in a professional capacity, then your estimate should reflect the fair market value for the professional service. For example, if a retired physician is donating two hours per week treating patients in your health clinic, the value of this volunteer service is significantly higher than $17.19 per hour. You could contact several physician offices in the community to establish a local fair market value of this service. On the other hand, if the same retired physician donates two hours per week to serve as a mentor for adolescents in your program, then the appropriate value for your estimation would be volunteer time at $17.19 per hour.

Take a moment to consider the potential impact of this in-kind contribution. If your program engages a local civic club to commit two volunteers for two hours (each) per week to your program, what would this total? The formula would be 2 volunteers x 2 hours per week x 50 weeks of annual program operation @ $17.19 per volunteer hour = $3,438. That's an impressive community match! The message: Don't overlook program volunteers. They provide valuable support to a program and should be reflected in the budget.

▶▶ *Budgeting In-Kind Contributions*

In-kind contributions are also referred to as "match" or "local match." We recommend using the term **local contribution** in grant budgets because some reviewers may not be familiar with "in-kind" or "match" and may become confused about who is paying for these budgeted items.

Our recommendation for presenting donations is to include these cost estimates in a separate column in your budget. In this method, your proposed budget would have four columns: (1) Budget Category; (2) Requested Funds; (3) Local Contribution; and (4)

Project Total. For each line item, column four would contain the sum of columns two and three. This method works very well for one-year proposals. The sample below illustrates a budget constructed in this manner.

Budget Category	Requested Funds	Local Contribution	Project Total
V. SUPPLIES			
A. General Office Supplies. Total cost estimated at $50 per month x 4 employees x 12 months (includes supplies such as paper, pens, tape, etc.). Lead Agency will provide supplies for 2 of the employees.	$1,200	$1,200	$2,400
B. Computer Supplies. Cost estimated at $100 per month per computer x 2 computer/laser systems x 12 months (includes laser toner cartridges @ $90 each, anti-static materials, disks, laser paper, cleaner, etc.); to be provided by Lead Agency.		2,400	2,400
Subtotal Supplies	**$1,200**	**$3,600**	**$4,800**

For multiyear grants, a separate column for Local Contribution is not feasible because separate columns are already required for each year of the program. One solution that we have used in large multiyear federal grant applications is to include a section in the project narrative addressing community support or local contributions. It describes the level of local commitment to the project and usually includes a list or table displaying specific contributions by source and estimated value of goods and services received.

The sample that follows contains excerpts from the narrative and a table from a recent Research Associates grant proposal.

Local Contribution: Our program will collaborate to maximize the use of local funds, in-kind (non-cash) services, and district resources as evidenced by the Memorandums of Agreements included in *Appendix B*. Our district superintendents, school principals, and other decision makers have agreed to integrate these local resources with the grant funding. Nearly fifty community, private nonprofit, business sector, civic, government, and faith-based organizations are committed to this proposal (*Appendix C*). The chart below and the Budget Narrative document the financial commitment by the school district to this project.

Resources Provided by Coalition	
Administrative Oversight: Project Director to oversee the five-district coalition (5% of Asst. Superintendent's salary at $70,000 = $3,500) + 5% of each Principal's time (.05 x $60,000 x 5 principals = $15,000) x 3 years.	$55,500
Payroll Support, Accounting, and Bookkeeping: Local school district will provide accounting, audit, and bookkeeping services at $10,000 per year x 5 school districts x 3 years.	150,000
Employment Advertising. Advertising for 5 administrative staff positions; cost estimated at $175 per ad x 3 major metropolitan newspapers x 2 Sunday editions.	900
Professional Development: Each school district Staff Development and Training Department has allocated local funds to focus on state academic performance standards, learning styles, and teaching methodologies at $25,000 per year x 5 sites x 3 years.	375,000
Educational Supplies: Educational supplies and curriculum not paid for by the grant at $5,000 per site x 5 sites x 3 years.	75,000
School-to-Work Coordinators and Adult Education Directors: Will be an integral part of the *SC CARES* program and will develop a career development program for students at an estimated value of $10,000 x 5 districts x 3 years.	150,000
Copies and Printing: $600 per site x 5 sites x 3 years.	9,000
Total Local School Commitment	**$814,950**

RA Secret! A word of caution about local contributions: Do not go overboard. If you show too much local support, the funding source or reviewers may conclude that you do not require their support. We recommend you provide evidence for in-kind contributions from 10 to 25 percent of your total project cost.

There is one other issue to keep in mind when deciding whether or not to include local contribution projections in grant budgets. For some funding sources, if the proposed budget includes local contributions, then these contributions are subject to audit. This creates additional paperwork requirements, so program management must make certain that audit trails exist.

> If your in-kind includes volunteer tutors, consider maintaining a log for tutors to sign to verify their presence on-site on a particular day and the total hours provided during that visit.

Indirect Costs

What Is It Really Going to Cost?

Indirect costs are costs incurred by the agency in administering the grant program, whether or not there is reimbursement for them.

Suppose, for example, your grant program employs five staff members and pays all of their expenses: salary, fringe, supplies, and travel. There is still additional cost incurred by your agency to employ these people. This includes the cost for the increase in the volume of work for the finance department as it monitors the funds, disburses paychecks, and provides tax records. In addition, at some administrative level, there will need to be someone in your agency supervising the project staff (or Project Director); this time is another indirect cost to your agency.

Typically, indirect costs are not reimbursed by grant funding. However, in some circumstances, the funding source (usually government) will allow an additional percentage of the grant award for indirect costs. The size of this percentage depends on the federally approved **indirect cost rate** your organization has negotiated. Private nonprofits, universities, and city or county governments are agencies that must have a federally approved indirect cost rate to qualify for this reimbursement.

> If your federally approved indirect cost rate is 10 percent and you are awarded a $200,000 grant plus indirect costs, then based upon total program costs, you would receive total funds of $220,000.

The RFP will be very clear as to whether or not the grant program you are considering will pay additional monies for indirect costs. However, novice grantwriters are sometimes confused by the concept of indirect costs. This stems from the use of two slightly different meanings for the term.

1. The first meaning (as introduced above) is when indirect costs refer to the negotiated rate your agency established with the federal authorities. This rate is supposed to reflect the cost to your agency for operating a grant program. Some funding sources will pay both the program cost plus an indirect cost to the agency for the program.

2. The second usage of indirect costs is simply the acknowledgement that it does, in fact, always cost the administering organization financial resources to operate a project. In this case, however, no one may be reimbursing the organization for these costs. They are simply absorbed by the organization (although they should acknowledged as a local contribution).

An in-depth discussion of the steps necessary to apply for a federally approved indirect cost rate is beyond the scope of this book. There are numerous resources available to nonprofits wishing to pursue this matter. You might consider reviewing the basic information available at **www.dol.gov/oasam/programs/ guide1.htm**. For additional information about determining indirect costs rates, go to your favorite search engine and enter "indirect costs."

▶▶ *Warning: Grants success can actually hurt your agency!*

Many nonprofits get into real trouble by failing to respect or provide for the impact of indirect costs. This usually begins when the agency has successfully obtained a few small grants. Encouraged by this success, the agency increases the number of programs it wants to implement and the number of proposals it submits. However, it fails to acknowledge that the administrative oversight required for each program is draining agency resources. Eventually, agency administrators are providing full-time grants management with no income to offset this expense. Plus, the administrators do not have the time to do their "real" jobs, the ones they were initially hired to perform. We encourage you to include administrative costs, such as a Project Director to supervise program operations, in your proposed grant budget.

Keeping It Real
Look at the Big Picture

Your budget totals should fit into a range you consider both appropriate for the scope of the program and acceptable to funding sources. While most grantwriters fear only asking for too much, we have actually heard of programs being rejected because they were asking for too little to accomplish their objectives! Thus, it is important you look at the big picture. We mean that you should consider your program objectives in relationship to both the activities you plan to undertake and your estimated total budget. Sometimes it may be helpful to estimate a dollar figure per client or per service provided to determine if your budget is reasonable.

Once you perform this review, chances are that you will need to make some adjustments to various line items. If your budget is too large—or too small—you will also need to reexamine your program strategies.

Many factors impact the cost estimates in your budget. In reality, there are many ways to justify costs that are actually much too high or too low to accomplish your objectives. However, we steadfastly recommend you prepare a budget that is reality-based and reasonably priced. *Never intentionally "pad" a budget or purposefully include unnecessary items or inflated cost estimates.* Reviewers will spot this immediately, and your proposal will not be funded. Instead, try to develop a well-funded program that can absorb some budget cuts if the funding agency reduces your funds.

RA Secret! One budget tip worth keeping in mind involves multiyear budgets. It has been our experience that budgets may reflect an increase of 5 percent per year to allow for inflation. We have successfully included these increases in both state and federal proposals, even when the guidelines suggest that program expenses must remain constant from one year to the next.

Putting It on Paper

Check, Recheck, and Check again

By now, you have seen a number of sample budget excerpts so you should have some ideas about our preferences for budget presentation. In summary, here are our budget recommendations:

➤   Always start the budget on a new page (if possible).

➤   Properly align the budget columns; a table format is preferred.

➤   Present main category titles in all caps, in boldface type, and numbered using Roman numerals.

➤   Assign letters to individual line items (or subcategories).

➤   Limit descriptive text to the Budget Category column only.

➤ Fully justify descriptive text unless it makes character spacing awkward.

➤ Right-justify the columns containing cost estimates dollar amounts.

➤ Express numbers in whole dollars only (no cents).

➤ Limit use of the dollar sign ($) to the first line of each budget page, subtotals, and the overall total.

➤ Present all entries on subtotal or total lines in bold type.

➤ Check and recheck your spelling.

➤ Double-check and then re-check all entries and totals. It is soooo easy to make an error. *(Believe us, we know!)*

RA Secret! Our last budget secret falls into the strange-but-true category. There is one word we recommend you never, ever include in a proposed budget. In our experience, it is a word that angers budget analysts and sends up psychological red flags to every reviewer. The word to avoid is **miscellaneous**. *Don't use it.*

In Closing: We have drafted all components of the proposal and developed a program-driven budget. In Step 10, we will look at our overall document for visual appeal as well as strength and consistency of writing style.

STEP 10
BRINGING IT ALL TOGETHER

After you have completed the tough tasks of developing and describing each component of your program, the real work begins. It's time to bring together these pieces—Problem Statement, Approach, Evaluation Plan, Management Plan, Sustainability Plan, Budget—into a well-ordered, attractive, easy-to-read, and error-free proposal.

It has been said that as much as 20 percent of a proposal score may depend on appearance. Unfortunately, too many grantwriters fail to recognize that the recommendations in this chapter are the most critical in determining whether they win or lose the grants game—sometimes by only a few points.

Here is what we consider in Step 10:

► **Structure:** Does your proposal's organization meet RFP criteria? If no organizational criteria are specified, are components arranged logically?

► **Concept Papers:** How do you structure a concept paper? What is included?

► **Writing Style:** Is your proposal clearly written, easy to understand, and interesting to read?

► **Visual Appeal:** Is your proposal attractive and does the format enhance readability?

➤ **Production Tools:** Are you using equipment that will produce a high-quality document?

➤ **Proofreading:** Is your proposal free of punctuation, grammar, spelling, and other errors and inconsistencies?

Putting the Pieces in Order

Hallelujah! It's a Proposal!

The grantwriter's first task in this step is to take all the grant narrative components, developed in Steps 3 through 9, and put them into the order suggested by the RFP. Now you have your first glimpse of the actual proposal—hallelujah! In fact, if your grant has been developed and written by various team members, this may be the first time the entire proposal is merged into one document.

➤➤ *Model Proposal Structure*

You may be developing a proposal for a funding source that provides no guidelines, or you may have an RFP that does not suggest an outline or any structured format for the proposal. If this is the case, we use an outline that is an appropriate submission model for most basic grant proposals. Of course, before your grant proposal is ready for submission, there will be other items to include such as table of contents, forms and appendices. We'll review those in Step 11.

A standard outline format is the best means of formatting proposal components, but only if that outline complies with the order suggested by the RFP. Usually, grants reviewers will be provided an outline by the funding source that follows the outline of the RFP. Therefore, reviewers will expect to locate grant components in specific locations. The outline that follows illustrates the order we use for the project narrative and budget if the RFP does not provide this structure.

I. Problem Statement

II. Approach

    A. Program Overview with Goals

    B. Program Activities

    C. Dissemination

    D. Sustainability

III. Program Goals and Objectives

IV. Evaluation Planning

V. Management Plan

VI. Budget

Keep in mind that this is a suggested model; we have provided the outline for those grantwriters who are seeking guidance. You may prefer a different order. For example, you may find it easier to include your evaluation planning in the Approach or in the Management Plan, which is fine. Structure your proposal in the manner that works best for your purposes, as long as you observe all requirements or suggestions that are contained in the RFP. The key is ensuring clear, logical flow for the reader.

▶▶ *Concept Papers*

What if you are writing for a foundation that has requested only a **concept paper** or a brief two-page overview of your project? Or, if you need to take an existing proposal structured for an RFP and rewrite it as a concept paper for submission to foundations and corporations? What should you include in a concept paper? How long should it be? How should it be structured?

First—and most important—You must still complete Steps 3 through 9 for any program you are planning. Each step is essential for understanding a problem and developing an effective proposal.

Then we recommend submitting a carefully constructed **cover letter** and a two- or three-page concept paper. A **one-page budget** may serve as a third page. Follow the guidelines below in developing the structure and content of these documents. (Research Associates offers a three-day seminar, **Certified Foundation and Corporate Grants Specialist**, for those who want to learn more.)

➤ **Cover Letter:** Your cover letter should be written in standard business-style format on your agency letterhead. We recommend including one paragraph addressing each of the following components:

- **Introduce your agency.** Tell the funding source who you are and where you are located, as well as what you do and whom you serve. This description may be based on your organization's mission statement.

- **Introduce the project.** The next paragraph is a brief big-picture summary of the project you are proposing. Pique the interest of the reader here; compel them to read the attached concept paper. *If you can't make them cry, at least make their eyes well up!* This paragraph should **briefly** address community need and the program goal.

- **Establish agency credibility.** Now convince the funder that you are worthy of their trust—and their money. This may be accomplished by several means. For example, mention your grants track record, name your board of directors, briefly offer evidence of fiscal stability, or describe ongoing programs. If you are a new organization, however, this can be difficult. Your best bet may be to attract some local community leaders to serve on your nonprofit's board. Another tactic for new agencies is to partner with existing agencies, allowing the financially sound organization to apply for the grant.

- **State the bottom line.** Let the funder know what the project will cost. There are several ways to do this: You may present the total project cost followed by the amount you are requesting (if seeking funds for only one component); you may state the project total and then list the amounts required for various project components (allowing the funder to chose a level of support); or you may ask for support for the entire program (perhaps mentioning in-kind agency and community support).

- **Close with a thank you.** Thank the funder for their consideration of your program and let them know you will be contacting them to discuss the possibility for funding.

➤ **Concept Paper Content:** The concept paper should be one to two pages long. None of these pages should be on agency letterhead. It can be helpful to call attention to the sections of the concept paper with the use of section headings. The readers who are scanning a stack of proposals will appreciate a clear presentation, and headings improve clarity. One paragraph should address each of the following components.

- **Problem Statement:** Your opening paragraph must succinctly capture the community need while compelling the reader to continue reading your proposal. So, begin with a "punch," if possible, to arouse interest. This could be a dramatic statistic or a heart-rending quote. However, don't rely merely on drama; also support your problem assessment with statistics from independent sources. Include a paragraph presenting statistics with the most relevance and the most impact. Be sure you have clearly explained the problem to the reader. Remember our recommended trio of sentences and incorporate them here: *The problem is ...; The problem is caused by ...; and Without intervention, thus and such will happen.*

- **Goals and Objectives:** A brief, clear presentation of your project goals and related objectives is necessary to establish the basis for your project activities. In the concept paper, you might consider a paragraph format or bulleted entries, if needed for clarity, rather than using a table to present the goals and objectives. Also, depending upon the size of both the program and the requested funding, it is not usually necessary to present the fully worded version of the objectives, specifying every qualifier. The accurate wording of your goal and a summary version of the individual objectives should suffice.

- **Project Activities:** In this section, you want to briefly present each of the major service-delivery components of the program. There is little emphasis on administrative tasks here with the exception of the planning and oversight committee or task force, which speaks to community involvement and support. This is also the section to briefly mention sustainability and evaluation, if relevant.

- **Management Plan:** It is helpful to include a paragraph addressing oversight of the project as well as a few key elements from the time line, particularly when you will begin providing services. Also consider outlining your evaluation plans, that is, who will be responsible, how information will be used, and how results will be monitored.

➤ **Budget:** Typically, your budget is presented on a separate page (also not on agency letterhead). Or, you may prefer to limit the financial discussion to the cover letter (the "bottom line" paragraph). This will depend on the size of your program and your request. Most of the time, an attached one-page budget, developed according to our recommendations in Step 9, will serve you well. A budget will further clarify program components and reflect positively on your planning and management skills.

➤➤ *Now what?*

Now that your proposal is assembled into one document, you must analyze document length. This holds true for either a full proposal or a concept paper. Compare the total length and the length of each component to any maximums specified in the RFP. Is it time to trim or to return for additional writing?

RA Secret! Most grantwriters who employ our Logical Grantwriting Model will find at this stage that they **must** begin to trim their proposal to fit within the allowed number of pages. If for some reason your proposal falls short of the maximum at this point, you may need to rethink your objectives and project activities because you may not have adequately developed and described the type of program anticipated by funders. We rarely submit a proposal more than one page short of the allowed maximum, and we believe this is another secret to our success.

Writing Style

Tips for Grantwriters

Writing style refers to how you express ideas. It is the result not only of the choice and arrangement of words but also the standards, guidelines, and conventions you follow. These choices determine whether your style is, for example, formal, informal, technical, clear, confusing, interesting, or dull.

What writing styles should grantwriters adopt? How important are word choices? What other issues should be considered?

By now, you should be aware that we emphasize the importance of clarity throughout the grant proposal. It is vital to your success that reviewers understand exactly what you are attempting to tell them. Thus, it is important that your proposal flow logically, with smooth transitions from one section to the next. Accomplish this by using transitional or linking sentences to ease the reader from one topic to the next. For example, begin your description of project activities in the Approach (or Program Strategy) with this sentence: "The information below describes our program components in more detail."

Based on our experience with many different reviewers, we have gained insight into other issues that can be helpful in terms of writing style.

➤ **Reading Level:** Write most proposals on a ninth or tenth grade reading level. This will ensure that your reviewers are able to read and understand your proposal without getting snagged by unfamiliar words and complex sentence structure. (Most newspapers are written on a sixth grade level.) If you are unsure about reading level, both Word and WordPerfect offer options that will determine the reading level of a section of text. (Note: The exception to this recommendation is a research or technical proposal that will be reviewed by professionals.)

➤ **Technical Language:** Avoid using technical language that may confuse the reader. Rather, write your proposal in layman's terms (again, except for research proposals). If you must use technical language, be sure to introduce or explain it to the reader.

➤ **Contractions:** Avoid using contractions (e.g., "is not" rather than "isn't").

➤ **Abbreviations and Acronyms:** Avoid abbreviations of proper names and undefined acronyms. Even if you define the acronym, a proposal full of alphabet soup is very difficult to read.

➤ **Slang:** Resist using slang because the reviewer may not know what it means. For example, don't write about teens getting "wasted" if you mean getting drunk. Having your proposal reviewed by a diversity of team members can be helpful in avoiding this problem.

➤ **Jargon and Trends:** Avoid jargon or trendy phrasing because it might not be understood—or worse, its overuse may irritate the reviewer. *We recommend you "think outside the box" here. Did you just cringe? Do you see our point?*

➤ **Sexist Language:** Avoid sexist language. It is grammatically correct to refer to a person of undetermined gender using masculine pronouns. However, "the grantwriter works hard for **his** money" may offend readers who consider this wording as sexist. We recommend applying plurality to resolve this issue. In the above example, substitute "grantwriters work hard for their money."

Also keep in mind that your choice of words is important in setting the appropriate tone in your grant proposal. As a reminder, we recommended earlier that two sections of your grant proposal should be written in specific tones: (1) the Problem Statement should be negative; and (2) the Approach should be positive and hopeful.

Here's another important reminder: Personalize your proposal. Write from the perspective that you live in the community. Write about **our** problems and what **we** are going to do about them. This will be hard for those of you who have learned to write in the passive voice and in the third person. But "Our children go to bed hungry" sounds much more urgent than "Hunger is a problem in the community." Also notice the use of the first person is plural. Your proposal should never include the pronoun "I"; rather, it is about our community, our problems, and our solutions.

▶▶ *Writing Resources*

It is an understatement to say that good reference books are important to every writer. At a minimum, the writer must have access to a good dictionary and thesaurus. Our latest find has been online at **www.Bartleby.com**. This website offers an impressive selection of great reference books online that are easy to search. These include The American Heritage Dictionary of the English Language, Roget's International Thesaurus, and other writing books.

In addition, there are two books we recommend, unconditionally, as helpful and necessary resources for the grantwriter. Any larger bookstore usually stocks these writing staples, and they are also available for order online.

▶ *The Elements of Style* by William Strunk, Jr., and E. B. White, is a small yet invaluable handbook. The fourth edition, published in 1999 and available in paperback, is a guide to the essentials of effective writing.

▶ *The Little, Brown Handbook* by H. Ramsey Fowler and Jane E. Aaron is available in several versions with recent publication dates. This comprehensive guide (nearly 1,000 pages) manages to be user-friendly while covering everything the writer needs to know.

▶▶ *Choosing Standards*

In our grantwriting at Research Associates, we borrow from the social sciences, adopting the APA Style developed by the American Psychological Association. We believe that the APA Style is easier to read, flows well, and is simpler than other choices. The ultimate APA reference is the *Publication Manual of the American Psychological Association*, Fifth Edition. However, APA Style and others (including MLA and Chicago) are presented in sufficient detail for the grantwriter in *The Little, Brown Handbook* and other writing guides.

▶▶ *References*

Let's consider documentation of references. We have already recommended, for example, that you include references for statistics in your Problem Statement as well as references to research in presenting the Approach. As a grantwriter, you should consider the what, why, when, and where of documentation (we've already suggested how: APA Style).

▶ **What?** Document every source from which you borrow information: books, professional journals, statistics, newspaper articles, website, or other sources.

▶ **Why?** Documentation tells the reviewer the sources of your information, thus crediting the author and avoiding plagiarism. Documentation also lends credibility to your proposal, demonstrating that you have done your homework.

► **When?** You must cite every reference within the text of your proposal. The APA format for citation depends upon factors such as the number of authors and whether the quote is direct.

► **Where?** Documentation should appear in two places in your proposal: first, within the text, and second, in a reference page at the end of your proposal that lists every source cited.

RA Secret! In our ever-constant battle against the constraint of page limitations, we never include the reference page or bibliography as one of the numbered pages of the project narrative. Rather, we include the reference or bibliography page as an appendix. In an exceptional situation in which the RFP suggests penalties for proposals including extras, we may even omit the reference page, but we always include reference citations within the text or insert a reference page or bibliography into a permitted appendix.

Visual Appeal

How Does It Look?

Once we reviewed a twelve-page proposal that was written entirely in paragraph style with no break in the text—not even section headings. Even though the topic was interesting (the law enforcement project was seeking funding for narcotics officers), it was still difficult to plow through the entire twelve pages without so much as an underlined word!

The appearance of your proposal will be enhanced by breaks in the narrative that add interest and white space to your document. You may interrupt the narrative by using text enhancements such as italics, boldface type, or underlining; applying formatting techniques such as bullets or tables; or by inserting graphic objects such as charts, graphs, or pictures.

Visual breaks and the effective use of white space will improve readability, help focus the reader's attention, and make your proposal stand out. Give your readers an occasional break by using the formatting strategies below.

▶▶ *Text Enhancements*

Text enhancements—italics, boldface, and underlining—are ways to emphasize and direct the reader's attention. They should, however, be used sparingly, consistently, and for specific purposes. Overuse will annoy and distract readers, and inconsistent use will be confusing.

Italics. We recommend using italics for the following: the name of your project throughout the proposal, whether it is the full name or a shortened version such as an acronym; reference to other major sections of the proposal such as the Approach or Appendix A; and situations such as book or magazine titles that are italicized based on standard practice. Long sections in italics can be difficult to read.

Boldface: This is used effectively for titles and headings and for calling out significant words or phrases you want the reader to notice. When overused, boldface can be distracting and lose its function.

Underlining. With the ability of word processors to highlight text using boldface and italics and other font selections, underlining is used less frequently than in the "typewriter era." You may find that an RFP specifies its use for section or subsection headings, in which case you should use it as indicated. Otherwise, use underlining sparingly.

Remember: You do not want to over-rely on these devices to convey emphasis or tone. This should be done primarily through your writing style, that is, the words you choose and how you arrange them.

RA Tip! The appearance of your proposal on your computer monitor can be very different from the printed copy. This difference will also affect the impact of text enhancements. Furthermore, enhancements affect fonts to varying degrees. Therefore, as you compare the effects of text enhancements in making your selections, be sure to base your final decisions on a printout—not the screen appearance—if your proposal will be submitted in print. (Electronic submissions will be addressed shortly.)

▶▶ *Formatting*

We recommend block-style paragraph formatting for the project narrative in a full grant application and the first one to two pages of a concept paper. In block-style formatting, paragraphs are not indented and are separated by a blank line. Uninterrupted, paragraphs, however, can be boring, and sometimes the clear presentation of information requires a different presentation. Consider occasionally breaking your paragraphs with lists and tables.

- ▶ **Lists:** Lists are used to present information in segments that are easy to read. They highlight the information presented by setting it off from surrounding text. This is helpful to reviewers who tend to scan. When using bullets with list items, avoid styles that are ornate or cute.

- ▶ **Tables:** We addressed the benefits of tables for data presentation in Step 3. Tables are an excellent solution for presenting large amounts of information, be it statistical, descriptive, or financial.

▶▶ *Graphic Objects*

Using boxes or frames, charts, graphs, and pictures is another way to highlight and simplify the presentation of information. Because insertion of these objects is a more intrusive interruption to the narrative, you should minimize their use in your proposal.

- ▶ **Boxes:** Putting a box or frame around text is a way to draw attention to an important point in your proposal. Consider boxing in your mission, goal, or other primary concepts in your proposal. Again, use simple, tasteful lines—no flowers or vines.

➤ **Charts or Graphs:** These objects can be helpful in presenting demographic statistics and trends in particular. They are an effective way to show comparisons between the target population and other groups. While we recommend using the occasional chart or graph, be sure to apply clear, accurate labels and other descriptors to these inserts. Poorly labeled graphs create confusion.

➤ **Pictures:** Pictures are rarely appropriate in a grant proposal. They are marvelous, however, for reports and thank-you notes to funding sources. Everyone loves pictures of happy clients! *For confidentiality protection, remember to get signed releases when using pictures.*

Graphic objects should be clearly identified; for example, "Figure 1" followed by a brief descriptive phrase. This also simplifies any references to an object. Remember also to introduce an object in the preceding text. The reader should never have to guess what information an object is presenting or why it has been included.

RA Secret! As a general rule, we recommend limiting tables and graphic objects to only one per page in a grant proposal. On the occasions when we have been forced (by page limits) to present two tables on one page, we aligned the side margins of both tables with the narrative margins. We believe this achieves a good balance between the positive effects of the visual break and the negative impact of technique overuse.

▶▶ *Other Appearance Choices*

A document's visual appeal is also affected by the writer's choice of font style, font size, margins, and line spacing. The proliferation of word processors has dramatically increased the options available to the grantwriter for each of these factors. The choices are, in fact, nearly overwhelming!

We recommend reviewing the RFP one more time to see if it requires or suggests (there is no difference to the obsessive grantwriter) any of these selections. We have observed a recent trend toward specifying a font style, font size, margin, and line spacing. (It's a fact that middle-aged reviewers prefer large, simple-to-read fonts with double spacing and one-inch margins.)

We recommend you carefully consider the visual impact of each of the following factors as you select formatting options for your grant proposal:

➤ **Font Style:** A font type can actually set the mood of the grant proposal, and unfortunately there are hundreds of choices available. While we would never want to go back to typewritten proposals, font selection is the Achilles' Heel of many grantwriters. We recommend avoiding fancy or exotic fonts in the narrative of your proposal. Stick with the research: It suggests that simple serif font styles are most pleasing to the eye. Our recommended choice is Times New Roman. One other factor to keep in mind is document length. For example, changing from Times New Roman to Arial font may increase document length by 12 to 15 percent.

➤ **Font Size:** The preferred font size for grant proposals is usually 12-point, and most funders who designate a font size chose this one. We admit that we often reduce our font size to 11.5 (unless the RFP requires 12) to allow us to insert more text into the designated number of pages. Thus, 11.5-point is the minimum font size we recommend for the narrative. (In an emergency, if you will be submitting all original copies and if the RFP does not state a minimum font size, you could go as low as 11-point, but we never said that!) Slightly smaller type is generally accepted in charts or graphs.

➤ **Spacing:** Line spacing is another factor that impacts document length. It has also gotten slightly more complicated with word processing. Remember when single or double was the only choice? The question today is, What is double-spacing? For a pleasing, double-spaced effect, we recommend setting line spacing at 1.5 or 1.6. (In fact, many documents look awkward with the line spacing set on 2.0.) When single-spacing is allowed, we recommend using a line-spacing setting from 1.0 to 1.2.

➤ **Margins:** In general, the margin should allow fingers to hold the document without covering the text. We recommend allowing one inch on all four sides of the document. This is considered a "standard margin" and is a good choice if you have no other guideline. However, we reduce margins when necessary to fit more text onto each page (when pages are limited). In this case, we reduce the margins all around to .75 inch, and **never** less than .625 inch. Because our text will be fully justified, all lines will be the same length, lending an even, pleasing appearance to the document.

➤ **Word Orphans:** A word orphan is a line of text that has one or only a few words. We recommend eliminating them during the final reviews of the grant proposal by rewording the preceding sentence(s). Word orphans are problems because they (1) skew the otherwise consistent spacing throughout your document; (2) create the visual illusion of extra spacing, giving undue emphasis to the break in the text; and (3) increase the total length of the document, which can be a problem with limited pages. Get rid of them.

➤ **Pagination:** Every page of project narrative in your proposal must be numbered. This is because grant proposals get dropped or copiers at the funding source break down and pages become mixed up. By numbering pages, you ensure that your proposal will be reassembled in the correct order.

Page numbering is one item that can go into the area reserved for the margin and is usually at the bottom of the page. We recommend indicating the total number of pages to provide reviewers with a sense of your proposal length; for example, "Page 1 of 20," centered and located one-half inch above the bottom edge of the page. We use the word processor's footer feature with margins set to match the text. Our footer might include the project title, left-justified, and Page x of y, right-justified.

Submitting Grants Online

An Easier, Quicker Method?

A relative newcomer to the grants development scene is online submission of the grant application. Some funding sources (government included) now allow the grantwriter to log onto a website and enter the application information directly. We believe that online submissions will be the grantwriting wave of the future, but this trend will probably not fully catch on for a few more years. Let's examine several issues related to electronic submission of proposals.

➤ **Do online applications save time?** Don't be lulled into thinking that this method takes any less preparation time, because it does not! You should **never** simply sit down at your computer keyboard, log onto the appropriate website, and simply "fill in the blanks." Even if you must submit your application this way, the full process of program development as detailed in this book should still be followed. Thus, your application components should be drafted and carefully polished to perfection **before** you log on to that website. In fact, many online applications will tell you which word processing program to use in preparing your application, so that it will "cut and paste" effectively during the online submission.

➤ **What happens to visual appeal?** Unfortunately, online submission can devastate your visually appealing document. Due to technical difficulties, it is not uncommon for the proposal text to lose all formatting codes during online submission. We have seen proposals printed after this has happened; it is not a pretty sight! Imagine your proposal with the headings and subheadings simply buried in the text, the text an uninterrupted flow of words—a grantwriter's worst nightmare!

➤ **What if you are forced to apply online?** We've read reports from grantwriters who adopted "emergency" formatting measures when forced to submit online applications. We don't necessarily agree with this tactic, but we know of one writer who used ten periods before and after each section header in an effort to help the sections of the grant stand out.

▶ **Do online applications ever work?** We have seen limited success within one division of a state agency that requires online applications. However, in this case, the application is constructed as a series of questions to be answered (or issues to be addressed). The responses are then submitted in text format, one response per question, which may include several paragraphs. This type of application does not really require other formatting techniques. The agency knows what they are expecting in each response category. In this case, the online application process seems to be working fairly well.

RA Recommendation: At this time, we believe the cons outweigh the pros for online submission of grant applications. Thus, we recommend that, given the choice, you should submit your proposal the old-fashioned way—printed on paper. This ensures you know exactly what the reviewers will be seeing.

▶▶ *Electronic Submission*

What about those applications that request—or require—you to provide a diskette with your grant application? Could this ever be a problem? Unfortunately, yes. In general, the funding agency is asking for diskettes to either (1) allow them to distribute your proposal to reviewers electronically, or (2) to print out additional copies of your proposal for various purposes, including distribution to reviewers. The funders probably naively believe that by simply asking you to submit your proposal in "Word" that there will be no problems. *Not true!*

As you may know, a print driver is the software that communicates between a computer and a printer. Each print driver will configure the same document (produced with the same word processing program) in a slightly different way, based on the specifications for the selected printer. Unfortunately, this "slight" difference accumulates until the difference for the document becomes dramatic. For example, text that once fit on five pages may now require five and one-half.

A technical writer reviewed a 25-page grant proposal for Research Associates just prior to submission. She had not yet installed our agency driver on her personal computer. When she opened the carefully constructed 25-page narrative on her computer, it became a 28-page document. Luckily, before she began cutting the document, she called us and we were able to deal with the problem.

What if the funding source printed our 25-page narrative using a print driver that caused it to be 28 pages long? If the RFP set a 25-page limit, we'd be out of the running through no fault of our own!

RA Recommendation: This one is a tougher call; we always try to accommodate the requests of the funding agency. Because of our concern for the document's appearance and the changes that printer drivers can produce, we suggest submitting only paper copies if this option is possible. While you cannot guarantee someone won't run copies (of copies, of copies) on a printer that needs a new toner cartridge, at least you will know your tables will make sense and your pages will fit within recommended maximums. If a diskette is mandatory, include a page before the document stating what program, font, and print driver were used to create the document. The reviewer will be inclined to use what you used, if available.

The Grantwriter's Tools
Striving for Extra Points!

Because we believe in striving for perfection to capture every possible point during review, we focus as much attention on our selection of tools for the production of the grant document as we do on every other aspect of grants development. We believe that you should, too. In this section, we review recommendations for selecting computer equipment and paper and making quality copies.

▶▶ *Equipment*

While it is true that winning grants may be churned out on manual typewriters, this is the exception and not the rule. As you are piecing together proposal components (possibly from different writers) and sending drafts back and forth to grant team members for review and rewriting, you do not need to be hampered by insufficient or out-of-date technology. We recommend you acquire—or arrange for access to—the best technology available.

▶ **Computer Hardware:** Start with an IBM-compatible computer with the most up-to-date components available. At the time of this printing, we recommend:

- Intel Pentium 4 processor, 2.5 GHz or higher
- 512 MB RAM and 128K cache memory
- 64 MB graphics card
- 80 GB hard drive (7200 rpm)
- Read-Write CD-ROM drive
- DVD drive
- 19-inch high-resolution color monitor (flat-screen)
- 56K-90V modem
- Windows XP operating system

▶ **Computer Software:** Grantwriters should have the most recent versions of WordPerfect and Microsoft Office with Excel, Word, and PowerPoint—and know how to use them all. Also be sure to install strong anti-virus and Internet security protection for your computer (Norton is good).

▶ **Printer:** Printer manufacturers are now rolling off new models every month. We recommend a laser printer with the ability to handle large files with graphics and to print 25 pages or more per minute. We prefer Hewlett-Packard printers with 32 MB memory and a large 500-sheet tray. Always buy extra memory for your printer, as this can greatly affect the printing speed.

▶ **Fax Machine:** Grantwriters must often rely on faxes to send or receive necessary forms, to share research, and sometimes to transmit edited versions of the narrative. If Internet links get interrupted, work can be faxed and used off-line until the Internet is available. The multipurpose, all-in-one machines that serve as fax, copier, scanner, and printer have become a useful tool for Research Associates grantwriters. When purchasing a fax machine, look at the bits per second (BPS) to determine speed of transmission. Typically, a 33 BPS or higher machine with a plain-paper tray will accommodate your needs.

➤ **Internet Access:** Get any high-speed DSL (Digital Subscriber Line) Internet or cable connection available locally and also subscribe to an Internet service provider (ISP) which may be accessed (dial up or DSL) from any site nationally.

➤➤ *Paper*

A good quality paper will enhance your proposal's appearance. Don't most companies use a quality paper for their business stationery? Well, we are recommending you do the same for grant proposals.

➤ **Weight:** Standard copy paper is 20-pound paper. For proposals, we recommend using a heavier weight, thicker paper: 24-pound bond. (This is not card stock.)

➤ **Color:** Traditional white is your best bet. Avoid all colored papers, brights and pastels, versus the normal 84 brightness.

➤ **Brightness:** You may not be aware that paper comes in different levels of brightness. (It's more than the color that makes you wince when reading a shocking pink letter; it's also brightness.) For white paper, brightness increases the appeal up to a point. We recommend using paper rated in the range of 90 to 92 for brightness versus a normal brightness of 84.

➤ **Printer-Specific:** Use paper specified according to printer type: laser or ink jet. This will produce higher quality results. Print your document using 600 dpi, but never higher.

If you are amazed that we make recommendations about your choice of paper, you shouldn't be. Paper weight and brightness make a difference in its appeal. If you are skeptical, we recommend that you print the same document on regular copy paper and also on our recommended paper and then place the documents side by side. One document will have more appeal. You will see it.

RA Note: The paper we use is Georgia-Pacific 24-pound bond with 90-brightness specified for laser printers.

►► *Copies*

Typically, funding sources ask you to submit an original application and also request a specific number of copies of the complete application, from forms to appendices. What do we recommend for these copies? And how should they be assembled? Our suggestions follow.

► **Submit all originals.** Print every part of the application on your good "grant paper." We even acquire or produce electronic versions of required forms so we are able to also print original forms. We want to ensure that the reviewer is examining the highest quality proposal possible.

► **Make necessary copies on good paper.** Some pages of your complete proposal may need to be copied. These may include signed forms and some appendices (to be discussed in Step 11). Of course, be sure your copier has been serviced recently and your toner is sufficient. And remember to put your good grant paper in the copier when making these copies. In fact, if you have a laser printer and an ink-jet copier, you will require a different paper for your copies than for your originals.

► **Mark one proposal as the original.** To avoid confusing the funding source, we still mark one of our printed applications as the original. You do this by stamping, writing, or word-processing the word "Original" in the upper right-hand corner of the first page of the application or by attaching a small note marked "Original." Be certain that this copy includes all forms with original signatures. Some RFPs specify the color of ink to be used for original signatures, so read carefully.

➤ **Bind each proposal copy separately.** Many RFPs will specify binding preferences. Recent trends are to avoid notebooks, folders, and covers. Also, many funders do not like staples (too permanent) or paper clips (too insecure). If your RFP offers no specific advice, we recommend using a binder clip on each copy of your proposal. Binder clips are available in a wide range of sizes; use the correct size. Binder clips will protect the integrity of each copy while allowing immediate release when necessary.

➤ **Assemble everything into one packet.** Place the marked "original" application and all requested copies into one packet or box for submitting to the funding source. We heard about novice grantwriters who submitted the original and each of three copies in separate mailings. This meant that their proposal was rejected four times, each time for not containing the required copies!

Proofreading

Avoiding "Misteaks"

Too many cooks may spoil the stew,
But too little proofing will backfire on you!

We cannot possibly say enough about the importance of proofreading grant proposals. We have heard repeatedly from our training participants who have served as grant proposal reviewers for funding agencies that error-ridden proposals are a major problem, and these are the least likely to receive favorable scores.

Before you submit any proposal, it should be reviewed numerous times by various reviewers to gain insights about different aspects of the proposal. You should consider training grants team members to identify strengths and weaknesses of your proposals. Your reviewers should be a diverse group representing different cultures and educational levels as well as various personal and professional backgrounds. Some reviewers should focus on grammar, consistency, and writing style. Others should focus on programmatic and budgetary soundness. Consider arranging for reviews by members of the target population to see if your presentation of the problem is valid and if the proposed program seems doable.

Despite the importance of having a proposal read and critiqued by others, some grantwriters avoid this review because they are not willing to accept constructive criticism. However, the only way your writing will improve is by learning from the suggestions of others. Our company's senior grantwriters all report that they enjoy getting their proofed work back from each other; it has always been improved or "taken up a notch." So, lower your ego and learn to enjoy!

RA Secret! Sometimes you get caught in a trap trying to implement conflicting suggestions from different reviewers. This is simply a challenge you must learn to overcome. For example, if two writers disagree about the wording of a sentence in your proposal, you probably should rewrite the whole sentence. Similarly, if you get snagged on a particular word or phrase, then you should probably look for other word choices. If your proofreader has to re-read a section more than once to understand it, you can bet that the reviewer will also have to re-read. To avoid irritating reviewers, do everything possible to ensure that your document reads well.

Here are some specific techniques you and your reviewers may employ to assist in your proofreading efforts:

► **Read aloud.** Consider reading the proposal out loud. This is a wonderful technique for reviewing the flow of your document. If you find yourself automatically rewording a phrase to make it "sound right," then it needs to be rewritten.

► **Read backwards.** To check grammar, read the proposal backwards, sentence by sentence (not word by word). This will stop you from expecting the next sentence to be worded in a particular manner or to say a certain thing.

➤ **Allow for a fresh read.** Use time to your advantage. Let your proposal "sit" between readings to allow for a fresh perspective. From experience, we know all too well that what sounds wonderful at in the early morning hours. (from a caffeine-induced high) often appears less appealing when read for the first time after a few hours sleep!

We cannot end our proofreading suggestions without mentioning the grantwriter's standard measure for proposal readability: the 7-11 Test. This comes from the supposedly "true" story about one grantwriting firm that always goes to the local 24-hour convenience store the night before a grant is due. Their mission is to have the night-shift clerk read their proposal. If the individual does did not understand it, the proposal is not ready to be submitted! We recommend that all grantwriters perform their own version of the 7-11 Test to ensure that your proposals are easy to understand.

RA Secret! Even at the very end of this entire grantwriting process, when we are placing the documents into the delivery packet, we have one final proofing step. We ask a calm, rested staff member (one who has not been racing around making copies or up all night rewriting some component) to thumb through every copy of the proposal, page by page, to make sure it is complete, intact, and legible. While it is embarrassing to admit how often we catch problems at this stage, it is truly another secret to our success.

In Closing: In Step 11 we address other components of your proposal that will be assembled in the final stages prior to submission. Truthfully, Steps 10 and 11 overlap and will be occurring during the same period of time. (No, that should not be the day the grant is due!)

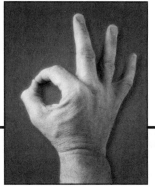

STEP 11
FINISHING TOUCHES

As your project narrative is being reviewed by various team members, rewritten and revised where necessary, and polished to perfection, there are some chores that must be performed before your grant application is complete and ready for submission. These tasks usually include preparing the application table of contents, writing a synopsis or summary of the proposal, assembling and labeling various appendices, and completing all required forms. Let's take a closer look at these components.

Table of Contents
That Section Must Be Somewhere!

Except for concept papers and small grants, we recommend providing a **table of contents** for most grant proposals even if the funder does not request one. It tells reviewers what information is contained in the application and in what sequence. A table of contents also serves as a last-minute checklist for assembling your grant proposal. A typical table of contents suitable for most grant proposals is offered below. We also recommend you provide the additional details for each section as described below.

Table of Contents

1. **Cover Page and Abstract** (if applicable)

2. **Required Forms**
   List every form that is provided in the application in the order of presentation.

3. **Project Narrative**
   List the primary sections of your proposal narrative, naming (at a minimum) each component of your proposal.

4. **Budget**
   Note: The funder may require its own budget form to be included in Section 2 with the other required forms.

5. **Appendices**
   List each appendix that is attached to your proposal.

We have also seen RFPs that require a separate table of contents for the project narrative. These typically must include page numbers for the project narrative only, since this is the section that is most likely to have page limits and page numbers. A table of contents for the narrative may be inserted immediately preceding the narrative and thus is especially helpful to reviewers.

Program Summary
The First Is Last

The **Program Summary** is exactly that—a summary or synopsis of your overall grant proposal, usually less than one page long. It is also referred to as the **Abstract** or **Executive Summary**. Some funders will require that the summary provide certain information, address specific topics, or follow a particular format; others offer no guidance. Typically, funding sources request a Program Summary as one of the first items in the grant application, although *it cannot* *be written until the full proposal has been developed.* Developing this section of the proposal first is a common mistake made by novice grantwriters. You cannot summarize what you have not yet written.

Reading research indicates that you have six to eight sentences at the beginning of a proposal in which to capture a reader's interest. With this in mind, we recommend that a Program Summary include six components presented in a brief yet compelling manner:

➤ **Goal:** A statement of the mission, goal, or overall purpose of the grant program.

➤ **Setting:** A brief description of the project setting and the target population and any compelling statistics.

➤ **Problem:** A concise statement of the problem(s) that your program targets and identifying why it is needed.

➤ **Program Strategies**: A summary of the program strategies that will be employed—a "big picture" approach rather than specifics.

➤ **Oversight:** A brief look at project oversight and evaluation plans.

➤ **Outcome:** A statement of the anticipated benefits of the program. They may include a restatement of the goal (how the world will be a better place) and could mention noteworthy exportable products.

We also recommend leaving the reader with a good feeling; this may be your best chance to engage the reader. It may be simple to blend your description of positive results (improvements in the community) with a positive feeling. A brief, compelling project overview combined with a "feel good" ending is the best possible Program Summary.

You may be uncertain about what we mean by "good feeling." Here is the closing paragraph from a recent Program Summary written by

Research Associates for a proposal whose name formed the acronym *RALLY.* Notice that it is a direct appeal to the reader for assistance.

Join with the district planners, administrators, community partners, and children of our community and help us create a better tomorrow. Let's RALLY together—for everyone's future!

Appendices
Squeezing in Extra Information

Appendices provide additional detail for your readers and are located at the end of the proposal. They allow you to expand the narrative beyond the page limitations and provide necessary information that is not appropriate to the scope of the narrative and would interrupt the flow of the proposal.

For example, the funding source may require you to provide a job description for the Project Director of your program. Rarely would it be appropriate to insert a full job description into the narrative when describing your project activities. However, it is simple to insert a reference to an appendix when you discuss the Project Director in the narrative as follows: (see Job Description in Appendix A). This parenthetical reference notifies the reader that there is a job description for the Project Director and also tells the reader where it is located.

▶▶ *Content*

Appropriate appendix attachments include items required by the funding source as well as supplemental information offered by the grantwriter for additional detail or clarification. Be careful, however, to follow the RFP and observe any stated limitations regarding appendices; current trends are for funders to limit appendices. Typical appendices include:

➤ **Résumés:** This appendix would include résumés and other information relevant to key personnel as required by the funding source. We prefer to provide a job description rather than a résumé, if possible, to avoid potentially tying the project funding to any particular individual. We do recommend, however, including the résumés for specific contracted personnel such as evaluators or workshop presenters.

➤ **Job Descriptions:** Job descriptions identify scope of work (description of duties); clarify personnel roles both supervisory and organizational; and define qualifications (education and work experience). Avoid using outdated job descriptions developed years ago. Instead, develop job descriptions for specific grant-related positions. (Research Associates offers a Directory of Grant-Related Job Descriptions available on CD.)

➤ **Organizational Structure Charts:** It can be helpful to illustrate the relationships between project personnel and regular agency personnel. Even more necessary are the lines of authority for key personnel when an oversight task force and an agency Executive Director share responsibility for grant management. (Whether or not this is included in the proposal, it should be one of the first implementation tasks for most grant programs.)

➤ **Partnership Agreements:** Typically signed by the Executive Directors of the partnering agencies, these documents establish the ground rules for the collaboration or partnership between agencies. With the current trend for grants funding to favor community partnerships, these are becoming more common in applications.

➤ **MOAs and MOUs:** Memorandums of agreement (MOAs) and memorandums of understanding (MOUs) offer evidence that community agencies have agreed to provide services for the grant project or participate in some other manner. This documented agreement among the local partners will substantiate your budget claim of local contributions. In this context, these agencies would not be considered full partners in the grant project, but rather as potential providers of services.

However, the terms MOA, MOU, and Partnership Agreement are used differently, and sometimes interchangeably, by different funders.

➤ **Letters of Commitment:** Letters of commitment and support can provide excellent evidence of the community's financial support, both documenting budget statements and indicating the community's receptiveness to the grant project. These letters will be discussed in more detail later in "Understanding Letters of Commitment and Support."

➤ **Certifications:** The most commonly requested certification is for the applicant agency's Internal Revenue Service designation as a 501(c)3 nonprofit organization. The applicant may also need to demonstrate that it meets local or state licensing requirements to provide certain types of services.

➤ **Data Collection Instruments:** Funding sources may request copies of any surveys employed during the needs assessment, or they may be interested in a summary of survey responses, item by item. Other relevant instruments would be any that have been proposed for use during implementation of the program; for example, pre- and post-surveys designed to measure changes in the target population.

➤ **Reference Page:** The Reference Page for documentation of citations, discussed in Step 10, is placed in an appendix to avoid being counted as part of the project narrative (which often is limited in page length).

➤ **Evaluation Schedules:** A time line indicating the components for evaluation is another item that may be simpler to attach as an appendix than to insert into the narrative. Don't forget to include reports to the funding agency.

➤ **Contractual Agreements:** If your project funds will be used to contract for personnel or other services, the funding source may want to see your standard agency contract for services. Some funders may request specific contractual agreements developed for the grant or, further, agreements already signed and in place provided the grant is awarded.

➤ **Required Forms:** Although most required forms are placed at the beginning of the application, some funding sources request specific forms in an appendix; for example, a listing of the Board of Directors or other sources of funding (not just for this grant but for daily operations).

RA Caution: Appendices can be the grantwriter's best friend and worst enemy. They provide an attractive alternative for providing detail that will not fit into the project narrative. Some funding agencies, however, do not distribute the appendices to grant reviewers; they are given only the project narrative. Further, some funders take away points if too much is attached (read the RFP again and again). For these reasons, over-reliance on appendices may be harmful to your proposal. We recommend that you keep this in mind and fully identify any appendix referenced in the narrative so that readers will understand its purpose and appreciate its potential—even if they are unable to actually view it.

▶▶ *Understanding Letters of Commitment and Support*

Not too long ago, grantwriters regularly added dozens of pages of community letters in an appendix to every proposal. Planners solicited letters of support from every possible source in the community and included them all. For a while, this practice was effective with funding sources. After a while, it seemed that funders began actually reading these letters and discovered, unfortunately, that few of them were meaningful. These were the generic **letters of support** from Agency A to Agency B saying that Agency B is a great agency, does good things in the community, and deserves this grant money (blah, blah, blah ...).

The current trend has been for funding sources to request and be interested in **letters of commitment** rather than letters of support. The distinction is that in a letter of commitment, the agency or person writing the letter offers or commits a tangible service or asset to the applicant agency. This committed asset may be included in the budget as a community in the appropriate line-item category.

All letters of commitment and support should be placed in one appendix. It still may be appropriate to include a few letters of support in an application to indicate the community's receptiveness to the proposed project, particularly if the sender is an acknowledged community leader. Most letters, however, should be letters of commitment to carry any real impact with reviewers. Here are a few suggestions for this appendix:

► **Sources:** Include a mix of letters from community organizations, local businesses, private nonprofits, politicians, civic organizations, professionals, and consumers.

► **Collection:** You cannot wait until the last few days in your grants development process to begin asking for these letters. We recommend that as early as Steps 4 and 5, once your model is drafted and your goals and objectives are clear, you begin seeking community support for your program and requesting letters of commitment.

► **Appearance:** Request that letters be limited to one page. While most should be typed on letterhead, a few letters handwritten in black ink from consumers can be powerful. In one of our funded early literacy grants, the grantwriter included a handwritten letter on notebook paper from one of the former program participants, a teen mother who was learning to be her toddler's first and most influential teacher. Her story "put a face" on the cause we were trying to sell, and her story made a compelling case for the need for grant funding.

► **Content:** Letters should be addressed to the applicant agency, verify the problem in the community, refer to the specific program by name, and say what the grant will do.

➤ **Involvement:** If the letter writer is serving on the planning committee or will serve on the task force, this should also be stated.

➤ **Support:** Letters should state that the writer supports the program and should also specify any assets or services the writer or agency will contribute. For example, "our agency fully supports this program and will allow the task force to use our conference room for weekly committee meetings as needed."

RA Secret! Grantwriters will be more successful in obtaining letters of support by drafting a sample letter and sending it out with the request for support. This is a timesaving technique for your community friends. At Research Associates we have also learned that we get much more specific and helpful letters of commitment when our sample letter offers a menu of suggestions for ways that community partners can support the grant program (aligned with suggestions in the RFP). We might include a list with twenty to thirty suggested items, depending on the focus of the project. These might include providing refreshments for a committee meeting, allowing students to shadow in the workplace, volunteering as mentors, having the company Personnel Director give workshops about employment applications, etc. In our experience, this menu "primes the pump," yielding letters from the community that actually commit resources to the program. This also makes each letter unique. *It is better to have no letters of commitment than to submit a stack of nearly identical form letters. Form letters may make your proposal "dead on arrival."*

▶▶ *Identifying Appendices*

There is nothing more irritating to the reviewer than paging through information that is not labeled or identified. This frustration typically occurs when the reviewer pauses in reading the proposal to locate an item (say a job description) and becomes lost in as many as fifty or more pages of various unlabeled appendices.

Appendices should be identified on every page. We recommend labeling appendix pages with an identifying stamp in the lower right-hand corner of the page. This strategic positioning ensures that the grants reviewer can leaf through the pages of the proposal and easily locate appendix material.

Appendices are typically identified by an alphabetic or numeric system. Thus, the first is Appendix A (or Appendix 1), the second is Appendix B (or 2), and so on.

> During our workshops, we remind our students that through the years we have made every mistake possible—and that our company's strength is in learning from these mistakes. Once we were preparing nine copies of a federal grant application that had an appendix over 100 pages in length. A graduate assistant helped by running all copies of the appendices on the good (i.e., expensive) grant paper to complete this part of the final preparation. She forgot, however, to stamp the appendices before copying them. So instead of hand-stamping 100 or so original appendices, we then had to hand stamp nearly 1,000 pieces of paper! We vowed to never repeat that mistake.

RA Secret! Because we continually strive to make our proposals friendly for reviewers, we prefer to provide a table of contents as the first page of an appendix containing multiple forms or other documents. For example, if an appendix includes MOAs with six different agencies, we would list each agency on the table of contents page for that appendix.

Required Forms
Don't Worry, Just Sign Here!

Almost every funding source that provides a structured application requests, at a minimum, a form identifying the applicant agency and a form summarizing the program budget. However, the quantity, quality, and appearance of forms vary widely, and grantwriters have to be prepared to do whatever it takes to figure out the forms required for their application.

While some corporations and foundations provide no forms and others have their own source-specific forms, many private funders now accept the Common Grant Application developed by the National Network of Grantmakers (NNG). This organization offers much helpful advice to grantwriters, and we strongly recommend you visit their website at **www.nng.org** or e-mail them at **nng@nng.org**. This group will also provide you with a different perspective for putting together a grant proposal.

Government funders have developed a set of forms commonly used by many national agencies. The good news about most federal forms is that despite their complexity, there is usually a straightforward explanation provided for every item on each form.

Although grant application forms have been available in PDF format for a while, most federal forms have recently been made available in both Word and WordPerfect versions. This allows the grantwriter to edit the information electronically, producing better, clearer forms. The website providing links to every federal agency's forms is **www.fedforms.gov**. This site is promoted as your "first step" to federal forms, providing one-stop-shopping for the forms most used by the public. The site allows you to search by U.S. agency or department as well as by strings, such as "grant" or "application."

▶▶ *Getting Signatures*

The completion of forms presents a classic dilemma to the grantwriter. On the one hand, most designated signers (such as agency directors or board chairs) prefer to sign forms that have been filled in completely. On the other hand, at least one form usually requires budget figures, and the logical process for grants development leaves budget totals and subtotals for program components until nearly the end of the grants development process. Woe to the grantwriter who must present the full application for approval at a regularly scheduled meeting of a nonprofit, government organization or school board before signature approval can be obtained!

RA Secret! At Research Associates, we designate one team member in the beginning of every grants development process who will be responsible for forms. This person develops a time line solely for forms and coordinates gathering required information from the RFP, funding source, grantwriting team, client agencies, and community partners to make sure that the forms will be ready in a timely fashion. This time line identifies a deadline for securing signatures on each form and when the forms must be in hand, signed, and ready for copying.

►► *Sample Forms*

The set of nine forms below is required when submitting most proposals to the U.S. Department of Education. They are included here because they share common characteristics with most other federal agencies and thus provide an overview of what the grantwriter might expect to encounter with any federal proposal.

1. **ED 424 Form:** Application Form for Federal Assistance. This form is used as the cover sheet for most federal grant applications and describes the applicant agency.

2. **ED 524 Form:** Budget Information, Non-Construction Programs. This is your budget form.

3. **ED 524 Form Instructions:** Budget Information, Non-Construction Programs. This explains the budget form.

4. **General Education Provisions Act (GEPA) Requirements, Section 427:** GEPA addresses issues regarding equal access and nondiscriminatory practices.

The certification, assurance, and disclosure forms below state that you will comply with all applicable federal laws as you administer your grant program.

5. **ED 80-0013 Form:** Certifications Regarding Lobbying; Debarment, Suspension and Other Responsibility Matters; and Drug-Free Workplace Requirements.

6. **ED 80-0014 Form:** Certification Regarding Debarment Suspension, Ineligibility and Voluntary Exclusion-Lower Tier Covered Transactions.

7. **ED80-0016 Form:** Certification of Eligibility for Federal Assistance in Certain Programs.

8. **SF 424B:** Assurances, Non-Construction Programs.

9. **SF LLL Form:** Disclosure of Lobbying Activities. This form is challenging because some interpret that if you don't lobby, you should not include it; recent interpretations tend towards including the form but leaving the content blank or marked "not applicable." We cannot seem to get a consistent interpretation on this!

►► *Single Point of Contact*

We could hardly complete our discussion of required forms without mentioning an extra grant application step required in nearly two-thirds of states: the Intergovernmental Review. According to the U.S. Office of Management and Budget, "Executive Order 12372, 'Intergovernmental Review of Federal Programs,' was issued with the desire to foster the intergovernmental partnership and strengthen federalism by relying on state and local processes for the coordination and review of proposed Federal financial assistance and direct Federal development." In plainer language, the original intent was for states to review federal grant proposals to prevent agencies from duplicating efforts. The order allows each state to designate an entity to perform this function: the Single Point of Contact (SPOC). (This process was formerly known as the A-95 Review.)

Different states interpret this review requirement in different ways: Some states require applicants to submit only Form 424, while others require the full application **prior** to federal submission. The SPOC then coordinates state and local inter-agency review of the application before submitting a report to the relevant federal agency. If your state requires SPOC review, then your federal application will not be awarded unless this step has been completed.

RA Tip! While most states dictate that grant proposals must be submitted to the SPOC prior to the grant deadline, many will accept the proposal within one to two days after the due date.

You can determine whether your state participates in the Intergovernmental Review and get contact information for your state at **www.whitehouse.gov/omb/grants/spoc.html**. We recommend you contact your state SPOC early in the grants development process so you can determine your local requirements and allow for time to comply in your grant development schedule.

RA Secret! When Intergovernmental Review is required and we must submit the full proposal to the SPOC, we protect ourselves by preparing a letter addressed to the SPOC stating the necessary information such as the grant program name and CFDA number and, of course, the date by which comments must be forwarded from the state SPOC to the appropriate federal recipient. At the bottom of this one-page letter we add the following: "**Proof of Receipt:** This is to verify that the above grant proposal was delivered to the State Single Point of Contact," with a signature, date, and time of delivery. We hand-deliver the proposal and get a Proof-of-Receipt signature on our copy of this letter. We then include a copy of this letter with our forms or appendices to verify compliance with the requirement in the application. Once, when the state SPOC failed to forward comments on time, we were able to prove that we had done our part by using this receipted letter. This small step in the process saved a grant that was nearly lost due to no fault on our part.

Grant Delivery

Getting It There on Time

At this point you have printed, assembled, and hand-checked every copy of the application. As we suggested in Step 10, your entire proposal ("original" plus all required copies) has been placed into one package for delivery to the funding source. Your proposal is ready to leave the nest!

Of course, you have checked and rechecked the RFP regarding delivery instructions to be sure you will get that proposal in on time. We have a few additional suggestions that might be helpful in getting that proposal submitted.

► **Package Identification:** Be sure you have addressed the package correctly according to the RFP. The return address should be the agency submitting the application, not the grantwriter (particularly if an independent contractor). It is also very important to clearly identify the contents of the package. For example, on a federal application, clearly write the name of the grant program and the CFDA number on the exterior of the package.

► **Importance of Timing:** We time the delivery of our proposals to arrive at the funding source around midday on the actual "due by" date. (Most RFPs state due by 5:00 PM on a specific date.) We believe this places our proposal near the middle of the stack of applications, the best placement for being reviewed. We don't want to be among the first proposals reviewed when reviewers are still grading conservatively, unsure of what to expect. We also don't want to be reviewed near the end of the process when reviewers may be tired. Of course, there is no telling how the stack will get split among reviewers, but we prefer the odds of arriving in the middle.

► **Hand Delivery:** If the funding source is local or within easy driving distance, it is always a good idea to hand-deliver your proposal. In this case, we recommend typing up a receipt stating "This is to verify that the *Whatever Funding Agency* received a grant proposal from *Name Your Agency on Date of Delivery.*" This receipt should include a signature line and a line to denote the "Time Logged In." (Make it easy for the funding agency to sign and date your document.) We may sound paranoid, but grant proposals do get lost; it has happened to us! Protect yourself with a signed receipt.

➤ **Delivery by the Postal Service:** Funding sources have gotten more stringent about rules for delivery by the Postal Service; for example, private meters are rarely accepted for proof of mailing. Also remember that the Post Office no longer routinely date-stamps mail, so if you are relying on this method, you must physically deliver your packet to a post office window and request a date stamp. At the federal level, some RFPs now suggest alternative delivery methods due to the security delays currently experienced by all inbound Washington, DC, mail. *If you do choose to mail via the Postal Service, print a receipt and ask the clerk to stamp and sign it for you—it can't hurt. However, we recommend avoiding regular mail service for delivery of grants since the sender is not able to track the delivery of the proposal nor ensure with certainty that the grant was received on time.*

➤ **Delivery by Private Carrier:** If we cannot deliver a proposal by hand, we prefer to use a private service such as Federal Express or UPS. And yes, we still have a prepared receipt that we ask the driver or clerk to sign (although some do refuse). These services do, however, assign a tracking number to your package that allows you to track its progress.

➤ **Double-Check the Delivery Date:** Some RFPs specify the date by which proposals must be received by the Postal Service or private carrier. Others state the date and time the proposal must be "in hand" at the funding agency. Be absolutely certain you are interpreting the date correctly.

➤ **Double-Check the Delivery Address:** We have seen RFPs with one address for hand delivery, a second address for postal delivery, and a third address for carrier-service delivery. So, always double-check that delivery address.

What now? Go home and collapse? No way! You have too much adrenaline and caffeine still circulating throughout your body. You might as well head to your office and try to clear your desk. It will take at least a day before you can calm down enough to succeed in the Grantwriters' Three Rs: rest, recover, and reintroduce yourself to your family and friends!

Post-Traumatic Grantwriter's Syndrome
No, You Are Not CrazyñYet!

In Research Associates' newsletter, *Grants for Education, Nonprofit and Government Agencies,* we published a humorous look at the desperate lifestyle suffered by grantwriters who are nearing grant deadlines and the aftereffects and associated maladies of this experience. The article, "Post-Traumatic Grantwriter's Syndrome," appears below.

Many grantwriters view grants development as a game in which the funding source has issued a challenge. For those of us who write grants regularly, this contest is exciting. Our competitive nature takes over, and writing a successful proposal becomes a battle with the victor receiving funding. For successful grantwriters, winning requires a balance of meeting the funder's expectations and requirements, developing a scientifically based program that includes proven program components, and incorporating what our customers want and need. A proposal that adequately addresses all these variables usually requires an extraordinary commitment of time and hard work. And it is in this commitment where danger lurks: grantwriting can become an obsession!

Once, when developing a model grant serving the homeless, RA President Mike DuBose worked four days straight without sleep. He found that ten caffeinated diet sodas combined with massive amounts of competitive adrenaline will pump the body into a "grant high" as the program model comes together and winning the game seems within reach. This is when grantwriters enter the Twilight Zone of Grants!

In the Twilight Zone, perfection becomes your number one priority, and the drive to win surfaces as you obsessively develop and constantly tweak your proposal to outshine other grantwriters. You strive to work harder, smarter, and more creatively than everyone else. You spend hours brainstorming ways to make your grant outstanding, winning extra reviewer points throughout. As the deadline approaches, your pace becomes more frantic. Every ounce of intellectual and physical energy is focused on your goal, and sleep becomes unimportant. Daily hygiene is limited to brushing your teeth and splashing cold water on your face. Your wardrobe of choice is pajamas and sweats. Family members are strongly cautioned not to enter the "grants room" except when delivering meals that now arrive in paper bags!

As you race toward your deadline, furiously formatting, cutting, and perfecting your grant product, you could watch the sun rise for the third or fourth day in a row, if you took the time to look out your window. Your phone rings off the hook as you exchange ideas with comrades and organize tasks, all in the name of grant perfection. Organization is critical as you ensure that all i's are dotted and all t's are crossed. With your brain whirling from a constant barrage of e-mail, you must force yourself to think logically. You try to convince yourself you are not tired. Surely your headache will go away if you drink just one more Diet Coke.

You have now reached the notorious "grant high"! Yet, you continue to feed your addiction with tremendous intellectual stimulation and occasional shots of caffeine and aspirin. Brain synapses are firing all over the place, and visions of $$$ dance in your head as you anticipate a lucrative visit from the Grant Fairy!

You race to the office to finalize your creation and print copies of the complete grant application. You carefully place the packet into the Federal Express package, jump into your car, and take off for the airport, hoping that God will keep the state troopers' attention elsewhere as you set new land-speed records near the airport. You enter the FedEx office and your grant is officially logged in and on its way to glory. Hallelujah! You made it with five minutes to spare!

Driving home, you realize you have only enough brain cells to hold the steering wheel and keep your body breathing. Your reaction time is nonexistent as your abused brain screams that there has been a firestorm in your head and you have burned out some connectors! Your body is shaking from sleep deprivation, physical inactivity, and poor nutrition! Those last two chocolate bars and the bag of fried pork rinds chased by Diet Coke seemed like a good idea at 3:00 AM.

Finally, you reach your driveway. Your recent addictions tell you it's still party time, but you can manage only a quick drink as you read through the final proposal, desperately hoping you will not see any typos. You reflect for a moment on your masterpiece and then it's off to bed–or the nearest sofa–and dreamland.

The next morning, your fatigued mind and body still crave the fix of constant activity. You are programmed to crank up your computer and review the dozens of e-mails that have become a daily standard, but there are none. The phone sits silent because most "regular" people, i.e., non-grantwriters, no longer want to talk to you; your recent obsession has alienated nearly everyone. Your spouse glares at you with an unspoken threat, indicating it's time for you to focus attention on your family or change professions!

In the following days, you receive a few mundane e-mails. The phone continues to be quiet. Like an addict seeking a fix, your mind screams for heavy doses of stimulating conversation about the subtleties of the RFP or the finer points of creative program strategies. You yearn for continuous rapid-fire e-mails. You wander aimlessly, feeling depressed. You find it hard to concentrate, and you sense your brain cylinders are misfiring. What could be wrong? Maybe you have the flu. Or worse yet, you might be coming down with some rare illness!

The malady just described is known at Research Associates as "Post-Traumatic Grant Syndrome." After a major grantwriting project, many of us experience these symptoms of withdrawal. We have pushed our bodies and minds to their limits, and now logic prevails, telling us we don't want to do that again at least, not soon. This illness can last anywhere from a few days to several weeks. However, symptoms immediately subside when you receive the long-awaited announcement that your proposal has been funded! Your grantwriter's heart, soul, and brain rejoice. It was worth it all!

On a more serious note, we acknowledge that while grantwriting is a great career, we urge you to exercise caution. As you hone your grantwriting skills, carefully monitor your stress levels. Actuaries who calculate insurance risks predict high rates of suicide among professionals such as dentists and accountants. We believe successful grantwriters tend to experience high rates of sometimes-unhealthy obsessive-compulsive behaviors leading to substance abuse, alienation, and divorce. We strongly recommend that you strive to eat properly, exercise, have some fun, spend time with your family, and practice your religious faith. Above all, take time for yourself; never jump straight from one project into another.

Now, has anyone seen my stash of Diet Cokes, chocolate bars, and fried pork rinds? I'm off to check my e-mail. I just heard that a new RFP has been announced!

What happens to your grant during the review process? In Step 12, we explore the grants review process and the role of political intervention.

STEP 12
FOLLOWING THROUGH

It is useful for grantwriters to understand what happens after their grant proposals arrive at the funding agency. Now we'll take a look at the grant review process and then consider two other important facets of developing a successful grant: responding to funding inquiries and the "art" of political influence—without offense.

The Grant Review Process
What Happens on Their End?

Several senior staff members at Research Associates have served in different capacities for various funding agencies. Our experience combines serving as a division-level grants coordinator for a governor, serving as a foundation director and on foundation boards, and reviewing grants for federal, state, foundation, and corporate entities. We have developed a description of the grants review process from the perspective of an agency that receives a moderate number of proposals for a competitive grant competition with a designated due date. Obviously, the volume of grant applications submitted to an organization will affect the level of organizational structure required to manage the review of proposals. We hope you will find this description helpful.

Typically, each grant application is logged in as it arrives at the funding source by date and time and then assigned a number. This process may be complicated if the funding source is receiving proposals for more than one competition and hundreds of applications arrive daily. At the federal level, these receiving sites are huge warehouses. In this case, the grant must be identified and sorted according to the program from which it is seeking funds. This is why it is important (per Step 11) that your CFDA number and program name are clearly marked on the outside of your grant packet. After being logged in, the first internal step will be an initial examination of the packets.

▶▶ *Initial Examination*

All proposals for any specific grant competition are accumulated as a group and then undergo an initial examination to determine whether the proposals will be accepted for the competition. During this exam, packets are opened and contents are compared against the basic RFP submission requirements. As a foundation director, one Research Associates vice president was responsible for overseeing the review of 300 to 400 grant proposals each year. Her experience led her to develop a stringent initial examination, enabling the foundation to weed out numerous proposals that did not comply with basic submission requirements and reducing the foundation's workload. The initial examination typically includes the following:

▶ **Cover Page:** The proposal cover page is checked to determine if it is correct, completely filled in, and includes appropriate signatures. If not, the proposal may be rejected.

▶ **Binding:** The binding is checked. If the proposal has been improperly bound (for example, inserted into a notebook against RFP rules), the proposal may be rejected.

▶ **Contents:** Proposal contents are checked. If the proposal includes extra items not allowed by the RFP (for example, video tapes), the proposal may be rejected. At the least, the extras will be discarded.

➤ **Forms:** Forms are reviewed to determine if any are missing or incomplete. If so, the proposal may be rejected.

➤ **Original:** The copy marked "original" is located and filed for safekeeping. If no copy is identified as the original, the proposal may be rejected.

➤ **Copies:** Copies are counted If the required number of copies has not been submitted, the proposal may be rejected. If copies were requested but not required, copies will be made.

Proposals that survive the initial examination are accepted for review, progressing to the next level for specialized review.

➤➤ *Specialized Review*

Copies are typically distributed initiating three separate tracks for proposal review: program specialist, independent reviewer panel, and budget analyst.

➤ **Program Specialist Review:** One copy of the complete proposal is sent to a staff person usually designated as the program specialist. This person is familiar with the program, understands the intention of the funders, and knows the RFP extremely well. *In fact, program specialists are often involved in writing the RFP.* They will review all components of the application including forms, program narrative, budget, and appendices. Depending upon the number of proposals, it may take many program specialists to staff one round of grant competition. Their tasks for the proposals assigned to their oversight are to:

• Perform a detailed examination of any non-budgetary forms for compliance.

• Focus on the program content and typically consider the following: Has need been demonstrated effectively? What is being proposed? Does the proposed program align well with the funder's intentions? Does the program seem likely to succeed?

- Briefly review the budget for a sense of "cost per service" and consider total costs versus the proposed scope of the program as well as the level of community support.

- Determine which proposals satisfy the intention of the funders and which ones appear to disqualify for the competition (and why). Program specialists may actually score each proposal using the reviewing criteria and form or they may informally rank their proposals in a priority order.

- Meet with other program specialists to discuss generalities of applications regarding scope of proposed projects, unique solutions, and range of estimated costs.

- Assess if there are any common problems that applicants encountered in fulfilling the requirements of the RFP. If so, they will try to determine the likely cause (for example, poor wording in the RFP) and decide whether the problem requires amendments to the instructions for independent reviewers.

▶ **Independent Reviewer Panel:** Independent review panels come in many shapes and sizes. Many federal agencies assign three to five members on a grants review team; this number may or may not include the project specialist. Often, reviewers come to a central or regional location, usually a hotel or convention center, where they stay for the week. Each panel will be assigned a number of grants to read, rate, and discuss (the number assigned is related to the length of the proposals). Sometimes reviewers are sent proposals prior to the meeting, and some reviews are conducted online. Whatever format is used, each independent reviewer is instructed to:

- Read each proposal carefully, focusing on program content with limited budget examination (in some instances, independent reviewers do not even see the proposed budget).

- Score each proposal according to a set of scoring criteria that may range from vague to highly detailed and specific. In addition, reviewers are usually asked to note both strengths and weaknesses of the proposal. These comments should support any extremely high or low scores.

- Meet jointly as a panel, sometimes with the program specialist or a committee chair, to determine an overall proposal score. This score may be an arithmetic average of the individual scores. In some panels, the low and high scores are discarded and the remaining scores are averaged. In other panels, if there is a spread between the individual low and high scores greater than some predetermined amount (say, twenty points), then the proposal must be discussed in depth and re-scored by each panel member. If there is still a large discrepancy, the program specialist or committee chair may intervene.

- Each panel generally agrees on one overall score for every proposal they review or their individual scores may be reported.

▶ **Budget Analyst:** The budget analyst will review all budgetary forms, other appendices such as job descriptions, and the proposed program budget (the copy of the proposal submitted to the budget analyst rarely includes the program narrative). *This is why we insist on including details, descriptions, and formulas in our proposed budgets. The budget analyst will review the proposal budget with the following types of questions in mind:*

- Do the numbers add up—vertically, horizontally, subtotals, and totals?

- Do the estimated costs make sense (are there explanations and formulas)?

- Do salary and supply estimates seem reasonable?

- Do estimated costs seem appropriate for the scope of services and the number of persons being served?

- Is the unit cost (or cost per consumer) cost-effective?

- Do you recommend this program as fiscally responsible and reasonable?

Budget analysts will then meet jointly to discuss general budget observations for the grant program, to identify any common budgetary problems, and to jointly review recommendations regarding funding and budget scores.

►► *Consolidation of Findings*

At this point, the recommendations of the program specialists, the independent review panels, and the budget analysts are jointly considered for the tabulation of a raw score for each proposal in the competition. These raw scores provide for the ranking of all proposals that will indicate the order of funding (highest score is funded first and so forth). However, these are not the final scores.

One other important step occurs at this point—and this one impacts you! There may be proposals that have scored high enough to be considered eligible for funding, yet there are problems with the application or questions about the program or the budget that must be answered before the proposal can continue to be considered. This is when the applicant named on the cover sheet will get a phone call from the funding source requesting more information. This call is both exciting—you are still "in the running"—and terrifying—they don't understand your proposal! (Later in this chapter, we'll make some recommendations for dealing with funding inquiries.)

After receiving responses to their questions, staff then assign raw scores to all proposals and compile the initial rankings of proposals. Next, these initial decisions must be reviewed by the "higher-ups."

▶▶ *Intervention "from Above"*

In almost every funding organization, there is a higher decision-making group with more authority than the program specialists and budget analysts providing the objective, non-political review—and certainly more powerful than the independent reviewers who may be paid or volunteer. The raw scores and initial ranking of each proposal will be considered by this in-house authority who often chooses to override recommendations and re-rank the order of the proposals prior to final funding decisions. After this review, scores and rankings become final. Welcome to the real world; this is where politics influence the grants process. We'll take a look at how you, too, can play the political game later in this chapter.

▶▶ *Funding Decision Announced*

The funding agency will now award grants beginning with the grant ranked as first (regardless of how many points it may actually have). Grants will continue being awarded based on the ranking until the money runs out. There are actually three categories of funding status:

1. **Funding awarded**. Hallelujah!

2. **Funding denied.** Boo hoo.

3. **Grant proposal "approved without funding."** This is the category that will break your heart. It does happen—we've been there. This seems to occur more often with federal funding, when there may be additional money available or funding is unexpectedly reduced. As a result, some proposals get designated in this terrible "approved without funding" middle ground. AAUGH!

RA Secret! Regardless of which of the above categories your proposal falls into, **always** contact the funding agency and ask for your reviewer scores and comments. It can be the most instructive thing you ever do as a grantwriter. We certainly never cease to be amazed by, nor stop learning from, our mistakes or the responses of reviewers. We also recommend you revise and resubmit a well-developed proposal at least twice before deciding that maybe it is time to re-think the problem and/or restructure the program.

Responding to Funding Inquiries

Keeping Your Cool!

It is about three weeks before the date that awards announcements are anticipated. The phone rings, you answer and hear "Hi, I'm calling from the DuBose, Davis & Black Foundation about your grant proposal." Now, before you shriek with delight, you might want to wait to find out why they are calling. Chances are good that a phone call at this time means the funding source has questions about your proposal. And we have some advice that can make a huge difference in what happens next in the life of your proposal, so keep reading.

Let us start by considering the dynamics of this phone call, because these are key to your ability to successfully navigate through this uncharted territory.

➤ **Power:** First, who has the upper hand and who has the power? Obviously, it is the funding source, and they will know this. Whatever they request, be pleasant and cooperative. After all, you are the one who stands to lose something here: your grant money.

➤ **Motivation:** Next, think about the task these callers are performing. Chances are good they have been given a large stack of proposals with various questions attached to each one. They have been instructed to call every applicant and get answers to all questions as soon as possible. Do you think they are going to want to accept any delays in receiving your answers to their questions? Probably not; they will want answers.

So, should you answer immediately. **Absolutely not!** In fact, try very hard to avoid giving quick verbal answers to questions during that call. Why? Because no one—not even experts like us—can think quickly enough to immediately provide the kind of answers that will save grants and keep budgets intact. In addition, you do not want the caller to interpret your answers incorrectly when reporting back to the funder's decision-making group. *(This advice is probably some of the most important offered in this book.)* So what do you do? Our recommendation is you try a maneuver we call the "RA Sidestep."

➤ **Plead for time.** First, stall, or try very hard to stall. You adopt a polite, helpful, even apologetic manner and explain as follows: "I am so sorry, but I don't have the authority to speak on behalf of our *grants planning team*. However, I can assemble them quickly, and we will respond to your questions very soon." If you manage to buy some time, you will be able to compose better answers to their questions.

➤ **How much time?** Next, you will need to politely negotiate for as much time as possible before your response is due. Begin with "May I have two days to respond?" If that fails, try 24 hours. If that fails try 5 PM today. Sometimes the caller may be on a tight deadline and is demanding or rude due to stress. *Remember: Always to be nice to the people who have the money!*

➤ **How to respond?** Now, you have to negotiate how you are going to respond; your real goal is to respond in writing. The reason is that with a written response, there is no quibbling about how the questions were asked or answered. So start by asking if you may send responses by two- or three-day mail carrier. If not, inquire about overnight mail. If not, ask for permission to fax or e-mail your responses. But always try to avoid responding verbally.

➤ **Write the questions down.** Write down the funder's **exact** questions so there will be no miscommunication with your grants team. And do a good job here; read what you have written back to the caller for confirmation that you have worded their questions correctly.

► **Answer the questions.** Once you have negotiated for some time, contact several of your sharpest team members and, together draft answers to the funder's questions. Your best approach will be slightly self-deprecating. For example, "We may not have been clear in the proposal, but what we meant to say was ... ." Then explain the concept again or differently, *even if you believe you were clear the first time.* You may need to reword. You may need to admit an honest mistake, but if it affects the budget, try to justify the money some other way. We encourage creativity and discourage dishonesty. You can achieve this goal.

Of course, if the funder insists upon verbal answers and/or immediate responses, you will comply because you know not to argue with funding officials. Right? R*emember who has the power.*

► **Submit your answers**. Finally, you will get your responses turned in on time, according to the agreement with the funding source.

The exception to the RA Sidestep is when the funders have a simple request, such as, "You forgot to include the addresses of the Board of Directors." In that case, you apologize and quickly send the missing item.

RA Warning! This telephone negotiation can be difficult. The funding agency will sometimes ask questions about things you have explained clearly in your proposal. You may want to scream, Did you bother to read my proposal? But you must maintain your cool. And if you are too hot-headed to negotiate this phone call, then you should not be the team member whose name goes on the cover sheet of the proposal as the contact person.

RA Secret! This brings up another point: never put your organization's chief executive as the contact person simply because he or she is the one with the authorizing signature. Most grant proposals want **both** an authorizing signature (the executive) and a contact person. This contact person should be the lead agency person most familiar with the grant. If you are a contracted grantwriter and not an agency employee, make sure the agency contact person on the proposal coversheet is at least on the grants team and also knows the RA Sidestep maneuver! In years past, we have had superintendents and nonprofit executive directors who were not familiar with the specifics of the proposal try to answer questions on the phone—and we lost some grants this way. Don't let this happen to you.

Political Intervention
The Art of Influencing Outcomes

We consider political intervention the art of influencing the outcome of grant competitions. Our goal is to influence—without offending—funding officials, and this is a delicate process. To accomplish this goal, we must recognize that relationships are the key to effective influence.

So how do you establish relationships with funders and politicians? How do you get your foot in the door? A simple approach is to identify an individual who either knows the funder personally or who worked in the politician's campaign. Surely somehow, somewhere, you already have a connection to someone who can help you get acquainted. So start trying to locate that individual. Inquire of your agency staff and agency board and ask them to ask their friends, neighbors, and relatives. Then, all it takes is a briefing session with your "new best friend" in which you explain the community need and your wonderful program. Then ask your new ally to request a meeting with their friend, the politician or funder.

If you cannot identify a contact for an elected official, then a cold call to the politician's local office is in order. Find out which staff person is responsible for grants, or more specifically the type of grant you are submitting. Connect with that staff person—in person, if possible. Now your foot is in the door!

Be prepared for this meeting. Know your facts and know your proposal. Plan to give them the cover sheet (identifying your agency and the grant program) as well as the Program Summary. Offer to provide the full proposal. You may ask if you may meet with the politician, but be grateful for the staff person's time. Keep in mind that you are not approaching them to complain about a problem; rather, you are offering a solution (your program strategy) to a problem affecting their constituents.

One question that comes up is whether this is **lobbying.** This is a concern because it is against the law to use federal money to lobby, and some of you may already have received federal grants. Even though you cannot lobby, it is always lawful to "provide information." You are bringing these politicians important information about needs in their communities and solutions to those problems—your program. Remember, you are not lobbying; you are providing information. And don't use federal funds to reimburse expenses, such as travel, while you are providing this information.

In our experience, politicians will respond to requests for intervention, particularly when they realize:

➤ **Benefits:** Explain the grant's potential benefits for constituents. Your role is to help them understand the community's need and the benefits.

➤ **Publicity:** By assisting with your proposal, they will receive positive publicity. Who can make this happen? You can, so be sure to demonstrate your capacity to do so.

➤ **Votes:** Their assistance may translate into additional votes—the true bottom line for every elected official! This is where you demonstrate community support for your proposal.

If you are going to manage an organization successfully, then building relationships and communication with power brokers will be instrumental to your success. Always work to establish and build these relationships and never fail to publicly acknowledge the help of every individual who contributes to your cause. Nonprofits need all the friends they can get. Nurture these relationships and in turn, they will nurture your organization.

Final RA Secret! This book, Developing Successful Grants, addresses the twelve-step Logical Grantwriting Model we teach in our three-day Certified Grant Specialist Seminars. It took you through all steps of program planning and proposal development right up to waiting for the grant to be funded. The next step is becoming a Certified Grants Administrator. This seminar covers the time period beginning when funding is announced and extends through basic program administration, oversight, and evaluation. Some excellent advice from that curriculum is a fitting close to this volume.

> **Do not spend any money until you have the funder's award letter or check in hand!**

Final RA Tip! If you need to decrease stress in your grantwriting life, use our guaranteed, no-fail exercise shown on the next page.

**For more information about Research Associates,
our other books and products,
and our grants development classes,
call us at (803) 750-9759
or visit our website at *www.grantexperts.com***

RA ANTI-STRESS EXERCISE

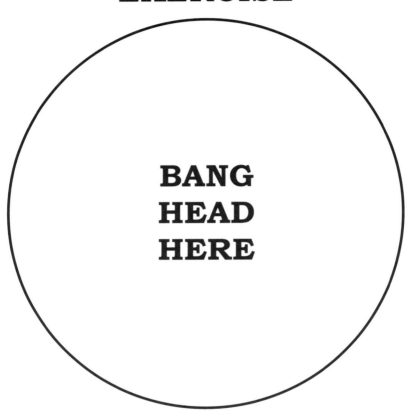

BANG

HEAD

HERE

Directions:
Continue to bang head
until anxiety dissipates!

GLOSSARY GRANTWRITING TERMS

ABSOLUTE PRIORITY: Conditions that must be met for a grant application to be considered for funding.

ABSTRACT: A written summary of the grant program from one paragraph to one page in length, usually written by the applicant. The Abstract, also known as an "Executive Summary," is sometimes used by the funding source as a press release to describe the funded program.

ACTIVITIES: Actions identified to achieve the objectives identified in a grant program. Several activities may be required to achieve an objective.

AGENCY: Organization providing services to clients or consumers, usually delivered by professional providers.

ALLOWABLE ACTIVITIES or COSTS: Project activities and expenses described in the program guidelines that can be included in the proposed budget.

ANNUAL REPORT: A report produced by a corporation or foundation presenting financial data and business or grant activities during the year.

ANNUAL PERFORMANCE REPORT: A report required by the funding agency and prepared by the grantee that can include a description of program accomplishments, progress towards program objectives, and budget information.

APPLICATION: The formal document submitted to a funding source describing the program and budget to be funded and often accompanied by supporting documentation. The application is generally the most complete presentation of the project and is often the basis for the grant agreement.

APPLICATION FOR FEDERAL ASSISTANCE: See UNIFORM APPLICATION FORM.

APPROPRIATIONS LEGISLATION: A law passed by Congress to provide a certain level of funding for a grant program in a given year.

ASSETS: Individual, association, and organizational skills, talents, gifts, resources, and strengths that are shared with the community and listed in the grant application.

ASSET-BASED INITIATIVE: An initiative based on the strengths of individuals and organizations that build a community's and grant project's capacity to thrive.

ASSET MAPPING: A process whereby a community's individual, association, and organization assets are identified and documented for community and grant building uses. A visual map of resources is usually created from the identification process.

AUDIT, FINANCIAL: An examination of an agency's accounting documents by an outside expert for the purpose of rendering an opinion as to fairness, consistency, and conformity within generally accepted accounting principals. Audits are generally conducted after the end of the fiscal year. Some grant programs require an audit of grant funds at the end of the project.

AUDIT, PROGRAM: A review of the accomplishments of a grant-funded program by the staff of the funding agency. A program audit may be mandatory or random; also known as "program monitoring."

AUTHORIZING LEGISLATION: A law passed by Congress that establishes or continues a government grant program; sometimes known as "enabling legislation."

AWARD: The formal, written document from the funding source informing an applicant that it will receive grant funding. Also, agreements including grants, subgrants, cooperative agreements, and contracts.

AWARDING AGENCY: The organization administering a discretionary grant award. See GRANTOR.

BENEFICIARY: A member of the target population for whom the grant was prepared. For example, a student attending adult literacy classes would be the beneficiary of a grant, while the school district would be the grantee. See also TARGET POPULATION, GRANTEE, AND SUB-GRANTEE.

BLOCK GRANTS: Grants from formula funds that are not allocated according to specific categories and are more flexibly distributed than formula grants. See FORMULA GRANT.

BOILERPLATE: An informal term referring to mass-produced materials or proposal components copied from other grant proposals. A word of advice: As the use of boilerplate material increases, chance of success decreases. Use of agency-written descriptions of common application components, however, is an effective time-saving technique and may be appropriate, for example, for an agency description or staff qualifications.

BRICKS AND MORTAR: An informal term generally referring to capital funds used for building renovation or construction.

BUDGET: The estimated cost of project activities.

CAPACITY: The potential for sharing assets, resources, gifts, and talents. To reach capacity, people and organizations recognize they are willing to share assets for community building and grant implementation.

CAPACITY BUILDING: Describes grants sought for the purpose of increasing or enhancing the scope of the recipient agency, e.g, funding new staff positions.

CBO: See COMMUNITY-BASED ORGANIZATION.

CDBG: See COMMUNITY DEVELOPMENT BLOCK GRANT.

CFDA (Catalog of Federal Domestic Assistance): Lists the domestic assistance programs of all federal agencies. CFDA gives information about a program's authorization, fiscal details, accomplishments, regulations, guidelines, eligibility requirements, information contacts, and application and award process.

CFDA NUMBER: Identifying number for a federal assistance program, composed of a unique two-digit prefix to identify the federal agency, followed by a period and a unique three-digit code for each authorized program. For example, all U.S. Department of Health and Human Services (HHS) grants are 93.XXX.

CHALLENGE GRANT: Grant used to stimulate additional fundraising by committing payment only if the grantee raises funds from other sources.

COMMUNITY-BASED ORGANIZATION (CBO): Nonprofit, non-governmental agency designed to work on a community-based project, need, or problem.

COMMUNITY DEVELOPMENT BLOCK GRANT (CDBG): The backbone of improvement efforts in many communities nationwide. CDBG monies fund activities that serve each community's development priorities, provided that these projects either benefit low- and moderate-income persons; prevent or eliminate slums or blight; or meet other urgent community development needs. CDBG is administered by the U.S. Department of Housing and Urban Development (HUD).

COMMUNITY FOUNDATION: A publicly supported organization that awards charitable grants in a specific community or region. In general, community foundations receive funds from many donors, hold them in an endowment, and use the endowment income to award grants.

COMMUNITY SERVICE BLOCK GRANT (CSBG): Grant program providing states and Native American tribes with funds to provide a range of services to address the needs of low-income individuals to ameliorate the causes and conditions of poverty. CSBG is administered by the Office of Community Services (OCS) under the U.S. Department of Health and Human Services (HHS).

COMPANY-SPONSORED FOUNDATION: A private foundation funded by a for-profit business but usually independent from the corporation and with its own endowment, e.g., BellSouth Foundation. See PRIVATE FOUNDATION.

COMPETITIVE GRANT: The program in which eligible applicants submit proposals. The proposals are then rated and ranked by the funding agency, and the highest ranked proposals receive awards.

COMPETITIVE REVIEW PROCESS: The process used to select discretionary grant applications for funding. Applications are scored by experts and those receiving the highest scores are considered for funding.

CONCEPT PAPER: An abbreviated form of the grant application, typically two to three pages, often used in seeking corporate or foundation funding. At the minimum, this paper should include a problem statement, program narrative, and budget.

CONTINUATION GRANT: Additional funding awarded for budget periods following the initial budget period of a multiyear discretionary grant.

CORPORATE FOUNDATION: See COMPANY-SPONSORED FOUNDATION.

CORPORATE GIVING PROGRAM: A grant-making program endowed and administered by a for-profit business; for example, BellSouth Corporate Giving Program.

CSAP (The Center for Substance Abuse Prevention): Provides national leadership in the federal effort to prevent alcohol, tobacco, and illicit drug problems.

DEADLINE: The due date for proposal submission. Funding agencies will specify the deadline as the date by which the proposal must be either received by the funder orcertifiably in the hands of the Postal Service or other approved commercial carrier.

DEMONSTRATION PROJECT: A type of grant project intended to establish or demonstrate the feasibility of new methods or new types of services.

DEVELOPMENTAL ASSETS: Forty internal and external experiences, opportunities, and qualities that young people need to be responsible, caring, and successful; developed by the Search Institute.

DIRECT COSTS: Costs directly associated with operating a grant program that are reimbursed by the funding agency. Direct costs typically include staff, consultants or contractual expenses, equipment, travel, and supplies.

DIRECTORY: A compilation of information about non-governmental funding sources including contact information, assets, restrictions, and application information.

DISCRETIONARY GRANTS: Grants awarded at the discretion of or based on the judgement of the funding agency to recipients selected in a competitive process. Discretionary grants usually involve a large number of competitive applications with limited available funding.

DISSEMINATION OF INFORMATION: The practice of sharing program outcomes with other impacted audiences. Dissemination is viewed favorably by potential funders since it allows their funding dollars to reach larger populations than the original project's target audience.

DIVERSITY: The many differences that make up communities and individuals, such as economics, culture, race, background, size of families, country of birth, talents/skills, and land natural environment.

DRAW-DOWN: The method by which a grantee requests payment from the funding agency. Frequency of draw-downs, also known as draws, ranges from weekly electronic wire-transfers to a single, lump-sum payment at the end of the project. Quarterly draw-downs are very common. Note: The verb is "draw down."

DUNS NUMBER: The Data Universal Numbering System (DUNS) number required for every applicant to apply for a grant with the federal government. The DUNS number is a unique nine-character identification number provided (at no charge) by the commercial company, Dun & Bradstreet.

E-APPLICATION: An electronic application system, allowing the applicant to apply for grant funding online.

ED: The U.S. Department of Education.

EDGAR: The Education Department General Administrative Regulations issued by the Grants Policy and Oversight Staff to provide ED discretionary grantees guidance in implementing program requirements with respect to program and budget issues.

ELIGIBLE ACTIVITIES: Specific activities authorized by legislation and for witch government grant programs can use available funds.

ELIGIBLE APPLICANTS: Entities or organizations permitted to apply for grant funding.

ELIGIBILITY CRITERIA: Standards that an applicant must meet to qualify as a grant recipient.

EMPOWERMENT: Recognizing and utilizing the power inherent in all people; usually means identifying and mobilizing this power for positive community change through a grant program.

ENABLING LEGISLATION: See AUTHORIZING LEGISLATION.

ENDOWMENT FUNDS: Funds intended to be invested in perpetuity to provide income for the continued support of nonprofit organizations. Endowment funds are generally held by foundations.

ESL: English as a Second Language.

EXECUTIVE SUMMARY: See ABSTRACT.

FAMILY FOUNDATION: An independent, private foundation funded by members of one family. See PRIVATE FOUNDATION.

FEDERAL REGISTER: Daily publication of the U.S. Congress providing, among other entries, public notice of all grants once they are approved by Congress.

FEDERATED GIVING PROGRAM: A joint fundraising effort usually administered by a nonprofit "umbrella" organization (e.g., the United Way) that in turn distributes the contributed funds to several nonprofit agencies.

FISCAL YEAR (FY): An accounting period (usually 12 months) at the end of which the books are closed for an agency, foundation, or governmental unit. Agency-wide financial audits are conducted after the end of each fiscal year. The federal fiscal year is October 1 to September 30.

FORM 990-PF: The IRS form required annually from all private foundations that provides for a public record of financial and grants information. Form 990 is the equivalent of a tax return for foundations.

FORMULA GRANT: A grant that Congress directs a federal department to make to grantees. The grant amount is established by a formula based on criteria written into legislation and program regulations, and awarded and administered directly by the department's program offices. For example, a formula grant from the US Department of Justice may require a state to allocate 75 percent of the grant to local law enforcement agencies and 25 percent to state agencies.

FR: See FEDERAL REGISTER.

FTE: See FULL-TIME EQUIVALENT

FULL TIME EQUIVALENT: The accounting term for the financial obligation for one full-time employee. Two half-time employees may appear in the budget as one full-time equivalent.

FUNDER: See GRANTOR.

FUNDING AGENCY: See GRANTOR.

FUNDING CYCLE: The schedule of events starting with the announcement of the availability of funds, followed by the deadline for submission of applications, review of applications, award of grants, issuance of contract documents, and release of funds. The cycle may repeat if funds are reappropriated or remain on hand after the first funding round.

FUNDING OFFER: A proposal by a federal agency, oral or written, to award a successful applicant a level of funding less than requested. This occurs when the agency either does not accept certain items of cost in the proposed budget or does not have sufficient appropriations to fund the project at the requested level.

FUNDING PRIORITIES or PREFERENCES: Objective factors used to award extra rating points to grant applicants who meet the established criteria. Also refers to considerations in funding decisions ensuring equitable geographic distribution of grant recipients.

GENERAL/OPERATING SUPPORT: A grant made to underwrite the general operating expenses or "good works" of an agency rather than for a specific project, for example, to pay rent and utilities.

GRANT: An award of money or direct assistance to perform an activity or project whose outcome is less certain than that from a contract.

GRANT AGREEMENT: A contract entered into by a grantee and a grantor. Typically based on the application submitted by the grantee, the grant agreement commits the grantee to carry out certain activities, within a stipulated time frame, for a specific amount of money. It often incorporates regulations that govern the use of grant funds. The Grant Agreement may include more restrictive conditions than were proposed in the application (or are required by law) and may be for less money than originally sought.

GRANTEE: The agency receiving the grant funds and the responsibilities of administering the program and fiscally managing the grant. Also known as the recipient. See GRANTOR and SUB-GRANTEE.

GRANTOR: The agency, corporation, foundation, or governmental unit that awards grants. Also known as the funder, funding agency, or grant maker.

GRASSROOTS: An overused term usually referring to community organizations run by people without professional expertise.

GUIDELINES: The directions explaining what activities an agency wants to fund, what applications must contain, how applications must be prepared, and how proposals will be reviewed. See REQUEST FOR PROPOSALS.

HHS: The U.S. Department of Health and Human Services.

HUD: The U.S. Department of Housing and Urban Development.

IN-KIND CONTRIBUTION: A non-cash donation of labor, facilities, or equipment to carry out a project. Typically, skilled and professional labor can be valued at the prevailing rate for the field. However, volunteer work performed by a professional or skilled laborer outside of their field is generally computed at some standard or minimum wage. See MATCHING FUNDS.

INDIRECT COST: Costs not readily identifiable with operating a grant program (also known as "OVERHEAD"). These are usually expenses related to administration and facilities; for example, the percentage of time that the Executive Director spends on a grant. Generally, indirect costs are reimbursed by the funding source only if an indirect cost rate has been negotiated and approved by the grantor.

INDIRECT COST RATE: A percentage established by a federal department or agency for a grantee organization, which the grantee uses in computing the amount it charges to the grant to reimburse itself for indirect costs incurred in doing the work of the grant project for example, the amount of time a bookkeeper funded by local funds spends providing payroll support to grant-paid staff).

IRC CODE: Internal Revenue Code.

INVITATIONAL PRIORITY: Areas of special focus the funder would prefer the applicant address in the proposal; e.g., emphasis on closing academic gaps between student subgroups. Typically, invitational priorities do not yield additional points for the applicant during review.

IRS: The U.S. Internal Revenue Service.

LEA: Local Education Agency.

LEAD AGENCY (Applicant): Represents a coalition or partnership of agencies joined to provide a grant program and serves as applicant and grantee. As applicant, the lead agency has the primary responsibility for submitting the proposal. As grantee, the lead agency is legally responsible for the program and has primary responsibility for administration and submitting all required reports.

LEAD AGENCY (Funder): The agency with the primary responsibility for approving or funding a project. The lead agency conducts the review, notifies other involved agencies, and issues the determination of the proposed action.

LETTER OF COMMITMENT: A letter that expresses the willingness of a community partner to commit resources to a grant project. The letter should offer specifics regarding the exact resources being offered, the terms of commitment, and the value of the services.

LETTER OF INTENT: A letter from a grant applicant to a funding organization expressing interest in a grant and summarizing a proposed program. The organization will use the letter of intent to determine whether to request that the applicant make a formal application for the grant.

LETTER OF SUPPORT: A letter that expresses the endorsement and encouragement of a community partner for a proposed grant program.

LEVERAGING RATIO: The proportion of grant funds to funds or non-cash donations or funds from other sources. For example, a leveraging ratio of 1:1 means that for every grant dollar awarded to a project, the grantee will secure one dollar from another source. The term implies that grant dollars are used to "leverage" other dollars. See MATCHING FUNDS.

MANDATORY GRANTS: See Formula Grant.

MATCH: See matching funds.

MATCHING FUNDS: The recipient share of the project costs and may be "in-kind" (the value of donated services) or "cash" (actual cash spent). Many funding sources will provide grant funds for only a percentage of the actual cost of a project; the grantee is required to pay the difference with money or non-cash donations from other sources. The non-grant funds are known as matching funds or the match. See in-kind contribution and leveraging ratio.

MATCHING GRANT: A grant awarded for the purpose of matching funds from another donor. See challenge grant.

MEMORANDUM OF AGREEMENT (MOA): A document providing the details of an agreement or understanding between two or more entities, signed and dated by authorized representatives of each participating entity. Often used interchangeably with Memorandum of Understanding (MOU).

MOA: See Memorandum of Agreement.

MONITORING, PROGRAM: See audit, program).

MOU: Memorandum of Understanding. See Memorandum of Agreement.

NEEDS ASSESSMENT: Determination of the needs of individuals, organizations, and communities, typically including those arising from poverty, adolescent pregnancy, drug abuse, depression, suicidal behavior, criminal activity, etc. They are almost always used to determine the need for new programs.

NOFA: See Notice of Funds Available.

NON-COMPETITIVE GRANT: Grant in which eligible applicants, pre-identified by the funding source, must simply complete necessary administrative or paperwork requirements to receive the award.

NONPROFIT: An incorporated organization in which stock-holders and trustees do not share in profits. The designated IRS tax status for nonprofits is 501(c)3. Nonprofits are usually established to accomplish some charitable, humanitarian, or educational purpose.

NOT FOR PROFIT: See NONPROFIT.

NOTICE OF FUNDS AVAILABLE (NOFA): Describes the amount of funds that are available and the conditions for award under a grant program. See REQUEST FOR PROPOSALS.

NOVICE APPLICANT: Those applicants who have not received a discretionary grant directly from the federal government within the last five years. (Note: Discretionary awards of federal funds competitively awarded as subgrants by states or other entities are not considered as discretionary for this purpose.)

OBJECTIVES: What is to be accomplished during the time of the grant project to move towards achievement of a goal, expressed in specific measurable terms.

ON SPEC: Informal for "on speculation." Consultants, including grantwriters, may do preliminary work "on the speculation" that if the project is funded more work will follow. The on-spec portion may be done for free in the hopes of securing additional work. This arrangement may raise ethical concerns with funding agencies.

OPERATING FOUNDATION: An organization whose primary purpose is to conduct research, promote social welfare, or sponsor other programs determined by its governing body. An operating foundation may make grants, but the sum is generally small compared to the foundation's own programs.

OUTCOME EVALUATION: Project evaluation that describes the extent of the immediate effects of project components, including what changes occurred. For example, measuring young people's knowledge of the dangers of drugs following their participation in an alcohol and drug curriculum.

OUTCOME MEASURES: Indicators that focus on the direct results of a proposed grant program on its target population.

OVERHEAD: See INDIRECT COST.

PARTNERSHIP: Two or more groups, organizations, or individuals joining together in a shared and mutually beneficial relationship working toward a common goal.

PASS THROUGH: The act whereby a grantee receives grant funds and disperses those same funds to a sub-grantee; generally a state sharing a percentage of grant funds received with local governments or other groups. It is common for the grantee to perform the program audit of the sub-grantee. A portion of the grant funds are often retained by the grantee to cover the cost of administration. See AUDIT (PROGRAM), GRANTEE, and SUB-GRANTEE.

PIPELINE: An informal term for grant applications that score well but fall just short of being awarded. If additional money is allocated to the program, or if funded projects do not materialize, a grant application "in the pipeline" may be funded.

PRE-APPLICATION: A condensed version of a grant application. A pre-application is submitted before a full application is prepared. It is often used by grantors to determine which applicants will be invited to submit a full application. See APPLICATION.

PRELIMINARY PROPOSAL: A condensed version of a full proposal. This may also be referred to as a pre-application. See CONCEPT PAPER.

PRINCIPAL INVESTIGATOR: This title is used most often in research grants for the person who will direct a grant project. See PROJECT DIRECTOR.

PRIVATE FOUNDATION: A nonprofit organization (usually funded from a single source) with directors or trustees that manage its programs. Private foundations typically award grants for programs that provide social, educational, religious, or other charitable activities.

PROCESS EVALUATION: Describes and documents what was actually done, how much, when, for whom, and by whom during the grant program.

PRO FORMA: Latin for "as a matter of form." The term is used to descride projected, proposed, or hypothetical numbers for a project, typically the budget.

PROGRAM INCOME: Gross income or revenue generated by a project. This may include fees, interest earned, funds collected through special assessments, and fundraising efforts. Program income may be subject to all of the conditions of the original grant award.

PROGRAM OFFICE: Conducts and/or coordinates the daily work of administering the grant program, including the review and ranking of applications.

PROGRAM OFFICER: An employee of a funder (government or private) who manages a specific program of grant funding and oversees grant competitions. Program officers also supervise and provide technical assistance to a particular funded grant.

PROGRAM REGULATIONS: See REGULATIONS.

PROJECT: The proposed program or plan for which grant funds are being requested.

PROJECT DIRECTOR:. The person who oversees the grant activity and is responsible for assuring the grant is conducted in accordance with all conditions and Federal regulations. Project Director typically describes a person directing a demonstration, training, or educational grant. See PRINCIPAL INVESTIGATOR.

PROJECT INCOME: See PROGRAM INCOME.

PROJECT PERIOD: The total time for which support of a discretionary project has been approved, usually in a series of one-year budget periods.

PROPOSAL: A written application submitted to a funding source describing a program and requesting funding for its support. Government proposals are more formal and are written according to the terms described in the REQUEST FOR PROPOSALS. Corporate and foundation proposals are less structured and may follow a preliminary letter of inquiry.

RECIPIENT: See GRANTEE.

REGS: See REGULATIONS.

REGULATIONS: For government grants, the documents containing the actual funding authorization and programmatic parameters established by Congress or state legislatures. Regulations include applicant and participant eligibility, nature of activities funded, permitted costs, selection criteria under which applications will be selected for funding, and other relevant requirements.

REPLICABILITY: The ability of a demonstration project to be successfully replicated (or repeated with positive results) in other settings.

REQUEST FOR PROPOSALS (RFP): A formal solicitation by a grantor seeking applications from potential grantees. RFPs describe what groups are eligible to apply (e.g., nonprofits and states); the background of the program; recent research; what each applicant is required to include in its application; how much money the grantor plans to award and to how many groups; the dollar amount in terms of the range of the awards; and other relevant information.

REVIEW CRITERIA: The standards and parameters used in the rating system employed to determine which proposals will be funded. Reviewers award points based on the applicant's ability to effectively, clearly, and creatively address the criteria.

REVIEW PANEL: A group of peers or experts selected by the funder to evaluate grant proposals in a grant competition and make recommendations to the funder on which should be funded.

RFA: Request for Applications. See REQUEST FOR PROPOSALS.

RFP: See REQUEST FOR PROPOSALS.

SECONDARY POPULATION: An identified group that may benefit from the grant program but is not the primary target. For example, a program serving high-risk youth may also provide some services for their families.

SEED MONEY: Informal term referring to one-time funds issued to start a new project, either as a grant or a contribution.

SERVICE PROVIDERS: Individuals and organizations that provide professional expertise to others as part of their jobs.

SOFT COSTS: Costs associated with a project exclusive of the personnel, equipment, and supplies cost of the project. Typical soft costs include consultant and legal fees, permits, etc.

SOFT FUNDS: Informal term referring to grant funds because they are not secure; that is, they are usually short-term and not repeating.

SPOC: Single Point of Contact; the state contact that an applicant must inform when applying for federal grants.

SUB-GRANTEE: A recipient of pass-through grant funds from a grantee and not directly from the grantor. A sub-grantee is held to all of the regulations of the original grant plus any conditions added by the grantee. Also known as "sub-recipient."

SUB-RECIPIENT: See SUB-GRANTEE.

SUPPLANTING: Deliberately reducing state or local funds because of the existence of federal funds. This practice is generally unacceptable in federally funded programs. For example, if an agency pays an employee from local funds for performing a certain job, but then receives a federal grant and begins to pay that employee from federal funds to perform the same job, this would be supplanting.

SUSTAINABILITY: The ability of program planners and managers to provide for program funding beyond the life of the current grant application. Funders often prefer to fund programs that exhibit this potential.

TARGET DATE: See DEADLINE.

TARGET POPULATION: The identified, intended beneficiaries (persons, organizations, communities, or other groups) of the services of the grant project.

TECHNICAL ASSISTANCE: An activity, generally utilizing the services of an expert, aimed at enhancing capacity or improving programs and systems or solving specific problems.

TRIPLE NET LEASE: A lease requiring the tenant to pay utilities, taxes, and insurance.

TURNKEY: An informal term generally referring to a project for which everything has been developed by a single source and which is ready for action or implementation. For example, in a turnkey grantwriting effort, a single grants consultant or organization provides all of the grants-development work for the client agency (i.e., locates a grantor, conducts a needs assessment, creates a research-based program, and writes the grant proposal application). The customer has only to "turn the key" to apply for funding.

UNIFORM APPLICATION FORM (SF-424): The standard, one-page form that accompanies all federal grant applications and which all applicants are required to fill out with basic information (e.g., name of organization, address, and contact person). The 500 series of federal forms include detailed budget information.

UNRESTRICTED GRANT: See GENERAL/OPERATING SUPPORT.

WHITE PAPER: An informal term referring to a literature review or research paper, often presented at conferences.

INDEX